THE NEW ASTROLOGY

ASTROLOGY

Taurus

BY
SUZANNE WHITE

The New Astrology

Taurus

A Unique Synthesis of the World's Two Greatest
Astrological Systems: Chinese and Western
By
SUZANNE WHITE

The New Astrology
Suzanne White

TABLE OF CONTENTS

What Is the *New Astrology?*

The New Astrology compares Western signs to Chinese signs and comes up with 144 *new* signs. If you are a Sagittarius and were born in 1949, then you are a Sagittarius/Ox. Simple. Take your regular, familiar astrological sign and match it with the animal sign of the year you were born. Now you have your New astrological sign.

Everybody has a dual nature. Some people are naturally greedy and grasping about money. But surprise! These same people can be generous to a fault in emotional ways, strewing sentiment and affection on their entourage like Santa Claus on a gift binge. People are complicated. They baffle us with their contradictory behavior. We even confuse ourselves with our own haunting ambivalences. How come you get along with Jack and care so much about him when in fact he gets on your nerves? Jack has an abrasive personality. You know that. But you can't help liking the guy. He fascinates you. Why? It's a dilemma. With a solution.

In order to understand your attraction for the difficult Jack, so as to comprehend the opacities of your own soul, by yourself, without the aid of a shrink or a psychiatrist, all you have to do is read *The New Astrology*, apply it to your day-to-day life, and you're off and running.

Why Does the New Astrology Work?

The New Astrology work attempts to help us understand human behavior within the universe through the "marriage" of occidental and oriental astrologies. By blending the western Sun Signs with the Chinese Animal signs, we can view many more sides of a person's character than we do with a single type of astrology.

The Chinese have divided time differently from us Westerners. Whereas we have 100-year centuries, the Chinese have periods of sixty years. We divide our centuries into ten decades. The Chinese divide their sixty-year spans into "dozencades" or twelve-year periods.

In the West, we divide our year up twelve times by its moons. Each 28- to 30-day month has its own astrological name. Every year our cycle begins anew. In the East, each year within the twelve-year dozencade has its own astrological name. At the end of each twelve-year period the Chinese cycle begins anew.

The twelve occidental months have celestial sign names: *Aries, Taurus, Gemini, Cancer, Leo, Virgo, Libra, Scorpio, Sagittarius, Capricorn, Aquarius, Pisces.* The twelve oriental years have animal sign names: *Rat, Ox, Tiger, Cat, Dragon, Snake, Horse,*

Goat, Monkey, Rooster, Dog, Pig. In both cases the astrological sign name refers to the character of people born under its influence.

So, in fact, everybody in the world has not just one but two main astrological signs. A Western "month" sign and an Oriental "year" sign. One sign is complementary to the other. Taken together, they show us more about the individual than either one can on its own. In the New Astrology, if someone is born in Aries and is also born in a Horse year, that person's New Astrology sign is *Aries/Horse.* Aries/Horses, as you will see, are not the same as Aries/Cats or Aries/Tigers.

There are 144 (12x12) New Astrology signs. Each is a combined East/West sign. The point of this exercise is to refine our understanding of human nature. Through the New Astrology we can learn to get along better with our friends, family and loved ones. We can find out why we tend not to harmonize with certain people. We can improve our knowledge of them, and of ourselves.

What is this book about?

This book is about **TAURUS.** All 12 kinds of Taurus. We begin with the Taurus/Rat and end with the Taurus/Pig. But before we discover all twelve types of Taurus, let's look closely at the Taurus sign's qualities and faults.

<table>
<tr><td rowspan="7">TAURUS</td></tr>
<tr><td>**Dates**</td><td>April 21 to May 21</td></tr>
<tr><td>**Ruler**</td><td>Venus</td></tr>
<tr><td>**Element**</td><td>Earth</td></tr>
<tr><td>**Quality**</td><td>Fixed</td></tr>
<tr><td>**Characteristics**</td><td>Ardor, Determination, Industry, Patience, Logic, Sensuality</td></tr>
<tr><td>**Sins**</td><td>Languor, Prejudice, Intractability, Gluttony, Complacency, Jealousy</td></tr>
</table>

Taureans never slap or sting. Rather, they creep up on you, affect you deeply and leave their indelible impression on your soul. Think of Taurus as a long sensual kiss. A huge tender bear hug. Or an eiderdown on a cold alpine night. Taureans are warm (but sometimes stodgy) customers.

Taurus people make excellent executives. They love money and enjoy earning piles of it. When a Taurus person gets rich, he hangs on to his money, investing it in sound stocks and bonds, building solid houses, and even storing gold sovereigns in a mattress. The key word here is *substantial.* Taureans do not have confidence in lightheadedness. Frivolity doesn't come naturally to them.

Many Taureans work with their hands. Even if a Taurus is a computer expert and seems more cerebral than manual, nine times out of ten there is a hidden craft or hobby lurking behind the scenes. Taureans enjoy forging beautiful things from natural materials. In fact, they are attracted to all sorts of beauty. Music thrills them. Flowers enchant them. The countryside seduces them. And art is their natural habitat.

Taureans are forever building their own workshops and renovating barns and old churches. They are not only home-loving, they like to get their hands into the cement and slather on the plaster, if only for the tangible joy of playing in the mud.

Taureans do not take kindly to sudden change. They like to be wherever they are supposed to be when it is time to be there. Taureans readily adjust to routine and for that reason make fabulous employees. Precipitous and unexpected events requiring flexibility and resilience may cause Taureans to dig in their hooves and refuse to budge. Bulls are obstinate and determined to hold their ground. It is wiser not to try to talk Taurus out of a sulk. Just let him paw the earth and snort and seethe on his own. Take a tranquilizer and a walk. Soon, when the inevitable becomes blatantly inevitable, Taurus will budge of his own accord, come out of his sulk and go with the flow.

Sensuality belongs to Taurus. Wherever there is pleasure you will find a Taurean plunk in the middle of it all. They love to bask in the "good life." Taureans cannot resist the tug of the opposite sex. When an attractive newcomer arrives on the scene, count on Taurus to see to it that the outsiders have a drink, are made comfortable and have slipped Taurus a telephone number or two.

Taureans are amorous and romantic without being flighty or maudlin. They are tender and don't mind public displays of affection. Love and all of its expressions appeal to the Bull. Taureans can be counted on to stray a bit where sex is concerned, but they never flaunt their infidelities and usually avoid sticky extracurricular entanglements. If you love a Taurus, feed him.

7

Now to the **Chinese Calendar and Signs.** Here is a mere sampling of the character of the Chinese Animal signs you will encounter in this book. For all the information on Chinese Animal signs please get my e-book THE NEW CHINESE ASTROLOGY© at: http://www.suzannewhite.com

The Chinese Calendar (1900 to 2020)

Year	Sign	Element	Year begins	Year ends
1900	Rat	Metal	01/31/1900	02/18/1901
1901	Ox	Metal	02/19/1901	02/07/1902
1902	Tiger	Water	02/08/1902	01/28/1903
1903	Cat	Water	01/29/1903	02/15/1904
1904	Dragon	Wood	02/16/1904	02/03/1905
1905	Snake	Wood	02/04/1905	01/24/1906
1906	Horse	Fire	01/25/1906	02/12/1907
1907	Goat	Fire	02/13/1907	02/01/1908
1908	Monkey	Earth	02/02/1908	01/21/1909
1909	Rooster	Earth	01/22/1909	02/09/1910
1910	Dog	Metal	02/10/1910	01/29/1911
1911	Pig	Metal	01/30/1911	02/17/1912
1912	Rat	Water	02/18/1912	02/05/1913
1913	Ox	Water	02/06/1913	01/25/1914
1914	Tiger	Wood	01/26/1914	02/13/1915
1915	Cat	Wood	02/14/1915	02/02/1916
1916	Dragon	Fire	02/03/1916	01/22/1917
1917	Snake	Fire	01/23/1917	02/10/1918
1918	Horse	Earth	02/11/1918	01/31/1919
1919	Goat	Earth	02/01/1919	02/19/1920
1920	Monkey	Metal	02/20/1920	02/07/1921
1921	Rooster	Metal	02/08/1921	01/27/1922
1922	Dog	Water	01/28/1922	02/15/1923
1923	Pig	Water	02/16/1923	02/04/1924

1924	Rat	Wood	02/05/1924	01/23/1925
1925	Ox	Wood	01/24/1925	02/12/1926
1926	Tiger	Fire	02/13/1926	02/01/1927
1927	Cat	Fire	02/02/1927	01/22/1928
1928	Dragon	Earth	01/23/1928	02/09/1929
1929	Snake	Earth	02/10/1929	01/29/1930
1930	Horse	Metal	01/30/1930	02/16/1931
1931	Goat	Metal	02/17/1931	02/05/1932
1932	Monkey	Water	02/06/1932	01/25/1933
1933	Rooster	Water	01/26/1933	02/13/1934
1934	Dog	Wood	02/14/1934	02/03/1935
1935	Pig	Wood	02/04/1935	01/23/1936
1936	Rat	Fire	01/24/1936	02/10/1937
1937	Ox	Fire	02/11/1937	01/30/1938
1938	Tiger	Earth	01/31/1938	02/18/1939
1939	Cat	Earth	02/19/1939	02/07/1940
1940	Dragon	Metal	02/08/1940	01/26/1941
1941	Snake	Metal	01/27/1941	02/14/1942
1942	Horse	Water	02/15/1942	02/04/1943
1943	Goat	Water	02/05/1943	01/24/1944
1944	Monkey	Wood	01/25/1944	02/12/1945
1945	Rooster	Wood	02/13/1945	02/01/1946
1946	Dog	Fire	02/02/1946	01/21/1947
1947	Pig	Fire	01/22/1947	02/09/1948
1948	Rat	Earth	02/10/1948	01/28/1949
1949	Ox	Earth	01/29/1949	02/16/1950
1950	Tiger	Metal	02/17/1950	02/05/1951
1951	Cat	Metal	02/06/1951	01/26/1952

1952	Dragon	Water	01/27/1952	02/13/1953
1953	Snake	Water	02/14/1953	02/02/1954
1954	Horse	Wood	02/03/1954	01/23/1955
1955	Goat	Wood	01/24/1955	02/11/1956
1956	Monkey	Fire	02/12/1956	01/30/1957
1957	Rooster	Fire	01/31/1957	02/17/1958
1958	Dog	Earth	02/18/1958	02/07/1959
1959	Pig	Earth	02/08/1959	01/27/1960
1960	Rat	Metal	01/28/1960	02/14/1961
1961	Ox	Metal	02/15/1961	02/04/1962
1962	Tiger	Water	02/05/1962	01/24/1963
1963	Cat	Water	01/25/1963	02/12/1964
1964	Dragon	Wood	02/13/1964	02/01/1965
1965	Snake	Wood	02/02/1965	01/20/1966
1966	Horse	Fire	01/21/1966	02/08/1967
1967	Goat	Fire	02/09/1967	01/29/1968
1968	Monkey	Earth	01/30/1968	02/16/1969
1969	Rooster	Earth	02/17/1969	02/05/1970
1970	Dog	Metal	02/06/1970	01/26/1971
1971	Pig	Metal	01/27/1971	02/14/1972
1972	Rat	Water	02/15/1972	02/02/1973
1973	Ox	Water	02/03/1973	01/22/1974
1974	Tiger	Wood	01/23/1974	02/10/1975
1975	Cat	Wood	02/11/1975	01/30/1976
1976	Dragon	Fire	01/31/1976	02/17/1977
1977	Snake	Fire	02/18/1977	02/06/1978
1978	Horse	Earth	02/07/1978	01/27/1979
1979	Goat	Earth	01/28/1979	02/15/1980

1980	Monkey	Metal	02/16/1980	02/04/1981
1981	Rooster	Metal	02/05/1981	01/24/1982
1982	Dog	Water	01/25/1982	02/12/1983
1983	Pig	Water	02/13/1983	02/01/1984
1984	Rat	Wood	02/02/1984	02/19/1985
1985	Ox	Wood	02/20/1985	02/08/1986
1986	Tiger	Fire	02/09/1986	01/28/1987
1987	Cat	Fire	01/29/1987	02/16/1988
1988	Dragon	Earth	02/17/1988	02/05/1989
1989	Snake	Earth	02/06/1989	02/26/1990
1990	Horse	Metal	01/27/1990	02/14/1991
1991	Goat	Metal	02/15/1991	02/03/1992
1992	Monkey	Water	02/04/1992	01/22/1993
1993	Rooster	Water	01/23/1993	02/09/1994
1994	Dog	Wood	02/10/1994	01/30/1995
1995	Pig	Wood	01/31/1995	02/18/1996
1996	Rat	Fire	02/19/1996	02/06/1997
1997	Ox	Fire	02/07/1997	01/27/1998
1998	Tiger	Earth	01/28/1998	02/15/1999
1999	Cat	Earth	02/16/1999	02/04/2000
2000	Dragon	Metal	02/05/2000	01/23/2001
2001	Snake	Metal	01/24/2001	02/11/2002
2002	Horse	Water	02/12/2002	01/31/2003
2003	Goat	Water	02/01/2003	01/21/2004
2004	Monkey	Wood	01/22/2004	02/08/2005
2005	Rooster	Wood	02/09/2005	01/28/2006
2006	Dog	Fire	01/29/2006	02/17/2007
2007	Pig	Fire	02/18/2007	02/06/2008

Year	Animal	Element	Start	End
2008	Rat	Earth	02/07/2008	01/25/2009
2009	Ox	Earth	01/26/2009	02/13/2010
2010	Tiger	Metal	02/14/2010	02/02/2011
2011	Cat	Metal	02/03/2011	01/22/2012
2012	Dragon	Water	01/23/2012	02/09/2013
2013	Snake	Water	02/10/2013	01/30/2014
2014	Horse	Wood	01/31/2014	02/18/2015
2015	Goat	Wood	02/19/2015	02/07/2016
2016	Monkey	Fire	02/08/2016	01/27/2017
2017	Rooster	Fire	01/28/2017	02/15/2018
2018	Dog	Earth	02/16/2018	02/04/2019
2019	Pig	Earth	02/05/2019	01/24/2020

RATS ARE:

Seductive • Energetic • Of good counsel • Charming
Meticulous • Sociable • Jolly • Persistent • Humorous • Intellectual
Lovable • Sentimental • Generous • Honest

BUT THEY CAN ALSO BE:

Profiteering • Manipulative • Agitated • Gamblers
Greedy • Petty • Suspicious • Disquiet • Tiresome
Destructive • Power-hungry

OXEN ARE:

Patient • Hard-working • Familial • Methodical • Loners • Leaders
Proud • Equilibriated • Reserved • Precise • Confidence-inspiring • Eloquent
Self-sacrificing • Original • Silent • Long-suffering • Strong • Tenacious

BUT THEY CAN ALSO BE:

Slow • Loutish • Stubborn • Sore losers • Authoritarian
Conventional • Resistant to change • Misunderstood
Rigid • Vindictive • Jealous

TIGERS ARE:

Hugely generous • Well-mannered • Courageous •Self-assured • Leaders
Protectors • Honorable • Noble • Active • Liberal-minded • Magnetic • Lucky Strong
Authoritative Sensitive • Deep-thinking • Passionate • Venerable

BUT THEY CAN ALSO BE:

Undisciplined • Uncompromising • Vain • Rash
In constant danger • Disobedient • Hasty • Hotheaded
Stubborn • Disrespectful of rules • Quarrelsome

CAT/RABBITS ARE:

*Discreet • Refined • Virtuous • Social • Tactful
Unflappable • Sensitive • Companionable • Solicitous • Ambitious
Gifted • Forgiving • Prudent • Traditional • Hospitable • Clever*

BUT THEY CAN ALSO BE:

*Old-fashioned • Pedantic • Thin-skinned
Devious • Aloof • Private • Dilettantish • Fainthearted
Squeamish • Hypochondriacal*

DRAGONS ARE:

*Scrupulous • Sentimental • Enthusiastic • Intuitive • Shrewd
Tenacious • Healthy • Influential • Vital • Generous • Spirited
Captivating • Artistic • Admirable • Lucky • Successful • Autonomous*

BUT THEY CAN ALSO BE:
*Disquiet • Stubborn • Willful • Demanding
Irritable • Loud-mouthed • Malcontent • Other-worldly
Impetuous • Infatuate • Judgmental*

SNAKES ARE:

*Wise • Cultivated • Cerebral • Accommodating • Intuitive
Attractive • Amusing • Lucky • Sympathetic • Elegant • Soft-spoken
Well-bred • Compassionate • Philosophical • Calm • Decisive*

BUT THEY CAN ALSO BE:

*Ostentatious • Sore losers • Tight-fisted
Extravagant • Presumptuous • Possessive • Vengeful
Self-critical • Phlegmatic • Lazy • Fickle*

HORSES ARE:

Amiable • Eloquent • Skillful • Self-possessed
Quick-witted • Athletic • Entertaining • Charming • Independent
Powerful • Hard-working • Jolly • Sentimental • Frank • Sensual

BUT THEY CAN ALSO BE:

Selfish • Weak • Hotheaded • Ruthless
Rebellious • Pragmatic • Foppish • Tactless
Impatient • Unfeeling • Predatory

GOATS ARE:

Elegant • Creative • Intelligent • Well-mannered • Sweet-natured
Tasteful • Inventive • Homespun • Persevering • Lovable • Delicate
Artistic • Amorous • Malleable • Altruistic • Peace-loving

BUT THEY CAN ALSO BE:

Pessimistic • Fussbudgets • Dissatisfied
Capricious • Intrusive • Undisciplined • Dependent
Irresponsible • Unpunctual • Insecure

MONKEYS ARE:

Acutely intelligent • Witty • Inventive • Affable • Problem-solvers
Independent • Skillful business people • Achievers • Enthusiastic
Lucid • Nimble • Passionate • Youthful • Fascinating • Clever

BUT THEY CAN ALSO BE:

Tricky tacticians • Vain • Dissimulators
Opportunistic • Long-winded • Not all that trustworthy
Unfaithful • Adolescent • Unscrupulous

ROOSTERS ARE:

*Frank • Vivacious • Courageous • Resourceful • Attractive
Talented • Generous • Sincere • Enthusiastic • Conservative • Industrious
Stylish • Amusing • Contemplative • Popular • Adventurous • Self-assured*

BUT THEY CAN ALSO BE:

*Nit-pickers • Braggarts • Quixotic
Mistrusful • Acerb • Short-sighted • Didactic
Pompous • Pedantic • Spendthrift • Brazen*

DOGS ARE:

*Magnanimous • Courageous • Noble • Loyal • Devoted
Attentive • Selfless • Faithful • Modest • Altruistic • Prosperous
Philosophical • Respectable • Discreet • Dutiful • Lucid • Intelligent*

BUT THEY CAN ALSO BE:

*Disquiet • Guarded • Introverted
Defensive • Critical • Pessimistic • F1orbidding
Cynical • Stubborn • Moralizing*

PIGS ARE:

*Obliging • Loyal • Scrupulous • Indulgent • Truthful
Impartial • Intelligent • Sincere • Sociable • Thorough • Cultured
Sensual • Decisive • Peaceable • Loving • Profound • Sensitive*

BUT THEY CAN ALSO BE:

*Naive • Defenseless • Insecure • Sardonic • Epicurean
Noncompetitive • Willful • Gullible • Earthy • Easy prey*

The New Astrology

TAURUS

ARDOR	LANGUOR
DETERMINATION	PREJUDICE
INDUSTRY	INTRACTABILITY
PATIENCE	GLUTTONY
LOGIC	COMPLACENCY
SENSUALITY	JEALOUSY

"I have"

Earth, Venus, Fixed

RAT

NERVOUSNESS	APPEAL
INFLUENCE	VERBOSITY
ACQUISITIVENESS	THRIFT
THIRST FOR POWER	SOCIABILITY
INTELLECTUAL SKILL	GUILE
CHARISMA	MEDDLING

"I rule"

Positive Water, Yin

Taureans born in Rat years benefit from a happy accident. Rats are often hyper. The Taurus mitigates the Rat's piano-wire nervousness. But to the lumbering Taurus personality, Ratso adds spice, pizzazz and a hefty pinch of calculation. The Taurus/Rat is a combination of William Shakespeare and the Ayatollah Khomeini: tough, bright, with nerves of steel and natural superiority.

It is the maintenance of well-earned position that essentially interests the Taurus/Rat. He likes power. But he doesn't necessarily want dominion over others. He can be ardent. But he will not step down from his pedestal of dignity to slobber over a love affair. I doubt that you will ever see a "sloppy" Taurus/Rat.

Taurus/Rats have enormous appeal and are capable of ruse the likes of which you are unlikely to encounter in any other sign. They are strong-minded and strong-willed. But rather than mashing on the accelerator in order to win the race, the Taurus/Rat may lean back in the driver's seat, ponder, then slowly, deliberately, deliver just the razor-sharp tactical stroke of genius necessary to come in first without even lifting a toenail.

Taurus/Rats make redoubtable foes. As they hardly ever seem to take anything personally and never exhibit their vengeances publicly, you cannot ever really tell what they're thinking. All you know is that they are thinking fast and effectively.

Taureans born in Rat years are walking file cabinets. They have infallible memories. What may seem like a petty detail to any normal person is, to the Taurus/Rat, a paramount fact. Complicated names return to their lips after ten years, as though they had seen the person yesterday.

The Taurus/Rat is definitely a master and not a slave. Yet, if need be, he can appear to humble, bat his eyelashes and even titter in his corner if he knows it's necessary to reach his goal. I will not go so far as to say he is ruthless—but almost.

Taureans born in Rat years are protective of those they care about. They can show enormous generosity toward people they want to help, although, being industrious by nature, the Taurus/Rat is inclined to help only those who help themselves.

The Taurus/Rat carries himself with dignity, behaves impeccably in company and appreciates good manners in others. It is obvious wherever he is that he is the one around whom everyone in his vicinity gravitates. Taurus/Rats look as if they have "got it together." But if you penetrate a bit deeper you'll note a hidden spark of fun lurking under the sleek façade. Unless you are part of the Taurus/Rat's select entourage, however, you may never get to share any of that playfulness.

Love

The Taurean Rat subject loves with the constancy and steadiness of an old stone wall. He or she is bound to be a highly sensual soul and for this reason may be given to occasional dalliance. But dalliance is not real life. And what interests the Taurus/Rat is bite-the-coin-real-honest-to-God-solid-to-the-core reality of LOVE.

If you love this person, be faithful. Don't try any funny business. Oh, you can be amusing and even a little light-headed from time to time. But you cannot be disloyal.

Taurean Rats are jealous and grasping and so involved in their relationship, so committed to the perpetuation of that unit, that any deviation seems to them perfectly implausible. So... if you have caught yourself a Taurus/Rat, stay close to home.

Compatibilities

I see you with a strong but gentle Pisces/Ox or Tiger. But you could very well couple with Cancer, Virgo or Capricorn/Monkeys and Pigs. The Ox gives you competition but you don't mind that so long as he doesn't thwart your power trip. Horses don't work for Rats, but you should particularly shun Leo, Scorpio and Aquarius/Horses. Cats are too cool to keep you fascinated forever. They exasperate you with their eternal reserve. Aquarius/Cats unnerve you the most. They're so calmly clairvoyant and laid back. You hate inertia.

Home and Family

The Taurus/Rat's home will be, first of all, traditional. Even if the lamps seem a little on the ultramodern side and the chairs smack of some posh up-to-the-minute designer's deft hand, look at the Louis XV commode over against the wall. And on its marble top? Copies of publications read only by top-drawer people with good taste in everything.

The family life will (even though Taurus/Rat is so frequently away at work) revolve around the Taurean born Rat member of the family. Bottom line, it is always up to the Bull/Rat whether the family summers in Maine or in Brittany. It's not exactly egomaniacal despotism, because Taurus/ Rat gives space to those he loves and allows room for them to measure up to very high standards. Let's just say that Taurus/Rats choose - benevolently but inevitably – to be boss.

A Taurus/Rat's childhood is meaningful in the extreme. You must first allow him to express opinions and draw his own conclusions. Taurus/Rats are frequently not the best students in the class. They are often bored by the triviality of school routines and prefer to approach study in their own steady, steely manner—independent of petty regulations. Frankly, Rat Taurean kids know the rules down to the ground. But they'd rather work out some system of their own, and often do.

Profession

Few professions are not open to this sturdy, bright nature. The Taurean born Rat is gifted for all jobs that require a strong sense of duty combined with exertion of power.

He likes money and is able to keep thousands of facts in his head at once and concentrate on at least five different pursuits at a time. Taurus/Rats are those people you see with four telephone receivers under their chins, signing documents on their desks and discussing a deal with a client in their office—multifaceted and not for a minute superficial.

As an employee, Taurus/Rat will only be biding his time till he can become the boss. This is a pragmatic person whose common sense far outweighs his urge for spontaneity. Taurus/Rats do make very hard-driving bosses, but their employees respect and like them and will rush around handing them things and making them tea. The natural superiority is undeniable in this character. He will always maintain dignity and keep a safe distance from his employees. But he's not afraid to smile and say thank you.

A few examples of Taurean Rats: William Shakespeare, Charlotte Brontë, the Ayatollah Khomeini, Studs Terkel, Charles Aznavour, Bono, Craig Sheffer, Irving Berlin, Joseph Haydn, Tchaikovsky, Tony Gwynn, Valerie Bertinelli, Zubin Mehta.

TAURUS	*OX*

ARDOR	LANGUOR	STUBBORNNESS	INTEGRITY
DETERMINATION	PREJUDICE	STRENGTH OF PURPOSE	BIGOTRY
INDUSTRY	INTRACTABILITY	ELOQUENCE	PLODDING
PATIENCE	GLUTTONY	STANDOFFISHNESS	DILIGENCE
LOGIC	COMPLACENCY	INNOVATION	BIAS
SENSUALITY	JEALOUSY	VINDICTIVENESS	STABILITY

"I have"

Earth, Venus, Fixed

"I preserve"

Negative Water, Yin

It would seem at first glance that the combination of Taurus the Bull and his soul mate, the ominous Ox, might indeed be born so unwieldy and ponderous as to sink into extinction at the age of two months. The opposite, however, is true. Taureans born in Ox years do tend to be big, heavy characters. But they endure.

Taurus is, of course, taciturn and grounded. Oxen, though eloquent and steadfast, are just plain slow. They take their time about life and go at each task as though it were coated in sticky paper. The key words with Oxen are deliberation and foresight. Closing the door can take quite a while. They take hold of the handle and push ever so gently but firmly, shutting the door panel without a sound and listening for the click that means it is soundly latched. By this time, most other people have been through five doors and out of the building.

No. This character is not in a hurry. Nor, therefore, is he impatient, hotheaded or impulsive. Taurean Oxen think first and leap into the fray after they've had dinner, a long sit and forty winks. As a result, they often make wise long-term decisions. Or at least considered decisions. Sometimes however, their wisdom (in the case of Hitler, for example) can be questionable.

There is little time for nonsense in the life of a Taurean Ox. She will appreciate poetry and enjoy watching ballet but she doesn't really feel she ought to take time away from her more serious work for such frivolities. Taurus/Ox is not a stuffy sign. Far from it. The sensuality quotient is high among Taureans of all persuasions. But the Ox/Taurus will he able to postpone his sensual requirements, delay his gourmet indulgences, stave off the raging desire for passion—because his first aim is to succeed and to gain fame and respect from his fellows. He's not striving for power over others. He is after power among his peers, esteem, admiration. Self-indulgence can wait.

I wouldn't like to be in a job competition with Taurus/Ox. If for one moment I let down my guard and did not stay up day and night to complete the project at hand I would definitely be the loser. Taurean Oxen can outlast anybody at almost any job that promises to take them a notch further toward their struggle's end. Of course there is no "end" as such. Taurean Oxen keep pushing ahead till they keel over and stop breathing.

This person will not be adversely affected by criticism. He may dress badly and forget to comb his hair. He may not shave for a few days while busy at some urgent pursuit. She may not bother to pluck her eyebrows or shave her legs. Again, the paramount motive is the goal.

For all his devil-may-carelessness about dress and grooming, the Taurean Ox can be both attractive and seductive People are drawn to his innate seriousness and ability to make others feel good about themselves.

Love

As we already know, cold-heartedness is one of Taurus/Ox's strong suits. If cornered by a lover or mate, this person is guaranteed to fight, and fight both hard and dirty. Taurean Oxen are capable of profound and somber love with regard to their paramours. But watch out for their cruel streak. It's always ready to clamp down hard on your heart and stay there for as long as it takes to demolish your equilibrium. Otherwise, as long as you don't try to outdo this sensuous creature, you may be rewarded with enduring and profound tenderness.

If you love one of these people, allow him or her to shine. Make room for this character to develop its slow but steady superiority and you will never have to weather a cloudy day. Don't, for Heaven's sake, ask your Taurean Ox to empty his or her heart of "feelings", or beseech him tell jokes and off-color stories at parties. If a Taurus/Ox wants to perform, he'll become an actor and rise inexorably to receive an Academy Award in his own sweet time. He does not need either urging or approval from you. He wants acclaim from the whole wide world.

Compatibilities

You'll not be bored with either Pisces or Cancer/Rats or Snakes. Roosters from these two signs please you, too. They are industrious, but still have "soul." I'd advise you to look into Capricorn and Virgos of the Rat, Snake and Rooster categories. They can be dour, but then so can you. You might try a Pisces or Capricorn/Monkey but only for brief flings. Give Leo, Aquarius and Scorpio of either Tiger or Goat families a wide berth. They are all too heady to be your steady.

Home and Family

Decor is not all-important to the Taurean Ox. As long as the surfaces are not too cluttered and necessities are more or less functional, this person will not rush out and order new furniture or fabrics so he can impress the neighbors. The Taurus/Ox's goal, remember, is achievement. Surroundings are only useful insofar as they assist him in reaching his goal. Oh, he will not live in a sty or accept to inhabit outrageously humble dwelling places. His self-image is in unusually good shape but nonetheless, he adores comfort. So a couple of deep comfy armchairs and a large oak desk with plenty of room for his papers and books might best characterize the Taurus/Ox's choice of backdrop.

With family, the Taurean Ox is not likely to be overly demonstrative. He will, however, tend toward the tyrannical and must be "handled". The kids will probably not be allowed to make noise while Taurus/Ox parent is toiling over some hefty problem. He or she will also be attached to earthy traditions and hope for offspring and/or siblings to share in this enthusiasm for things natural.

As a kid, the Taurean Ox will likely spend quite a lot of time on his own. He won't be completely solitary. But he will always prefer the company of his cronies to that of his parents or brothers and sisters. When his talents lean toward the artistic, he must be encouraged. Whatever he does choose to pursue—a sport, mastery of a musical instrument or the ballet, he has the innate strength of purpose to persevere and excel.

Profession

Jack Nicholson, a famous Taurus/Ox actor, said recently in a newspaper interview that he felt there was no such thing as "the best age" for success and happiness. He claimed that one should feel good about oneself at all ages and that achievement ought never to depend upon something so transient as "youth" or "beauty" or "charm."

This attitude is typical of the Taurean Ox personality. In work situations, no matter what a Taurus/Ox is aiming for, there is no substitute in his mind for hard work, diligence and might. Age shouldn't have anything to do with it. Nor, according to the Taurean Ox's workaholic creed, should any trifles such as ethnic background, social position or, God forbid, sexual attraction! prevent success.

What can a Taurean Ox do for a living? Answer: anything, as long as it's not insignificant. These natives should be guided into careers where tenacity and drive get you furthest. They might choose athlete, reporter, salesperson, actor, musician or researcher.

Famous Taurus/Oxen: Adolf Hitler, Gary Cooper, Billy Joel, Dennis Rodman, Enya, Gary Cooper, George Clooney, Isiah Thomas, Jack Nicholson, Joël and Jean-Pierre Beltoise, Ludwig Wittgenstein, Madeleine Albright, Saddam Hussein, Tim Roth, Véronique Sanson.

TAURUS		TIGER	

ARDOR	LANGUOR	FERVOR	IMPETUOSITY
DETERMINATION	PREJUDICE	BRAVERY	HOTHEADEDNESS
INDUSTRY	INTRACTABILITY	MAGNETISM	DISOBEDIENCE
PATIENCE	GLUTTONY	GOODLUCK	SWAGGER
LOGIC	COMPLACENCY	BENEVOLENCE	INTEMPERANCE
SENSUALITY	JEALOUSY	AUTHORITY	ITINERANCY

"I have"

Earth, Venus, Fixed

"I watch"

Positive Wood, Yang

Here is the down-to-earth Tiger, the only Tiger who manages to keep all four paws on the ground and his head together at the same time. A steadier Tiger. A more vigilant Taurus.

The mind of the Taurean born Tiger is both tight and shipshape. Nothing that enters there gets out the other side without being carefully recorded. Tigers like to experience new things. Taureans want to keep everything. The combination results in a redoubtably savvy character who, although he may seem slightly eccentric and just a smidgen too easygoing, is really keeping score while you're busy watching the grass grow.

All in all, the Taurus/Tiger is a serious person. There may be something lighthearted in his manner, a certain jauntiness in his gait, a twinkle in the eye. But don't be fooled. The Tiger born Taurus never really lets down his guard. He's wily and he's wary. He's capable and truly enjoys leading. Don't attempt to get ahead of this creature or he'll be likely to pounce.

Tiger Taurean people are rarely haughty. She may be the Queen of England (as it just so happens) but she doesn't have much pretense or snobbery about her. These people favor simple pleasures.

Tigers born in Taurus love crowds. They don't have to be the center of attention, yet they get a kick out of watching others perform without feeling ego-threatened. This subject possesses natural nobility. It comes with the territory. Taurus/Tigers are modest people who plod with panache.

The Taurus/Tiger loves to be mobile. Ask him or her to take a trip tomorrow and the bags will be packed before you can buy the tickets, They are gregarious in a pleasant, settled way, and can be taken absolutely anywhere. They have excellent manners and good common sense about the polite pose to strike in any given company.

Tigers born in Taurus are far from perfect. They tend to excessive individuality. It can be unnerving. Taurean Tigers like things their way and see no reason why they cannot have their druthers. They are the kind of people who will prefer some cheap but exotic tea drink from Lisbon where they were once stranded overnight, to the best champagne money can buy. They may show up at your house for lunch with a quart of ice cream, which they will insist on eating instead of your painstakingly-prepared soup and salad. They don't care what anybody thinks.

Taurean Tigers may be able to get along on very little money. Their needs can he pared down to the barest essentials. They don't mind if you want to spend a cool million dollars a year. They mostly prefer to keep expenses down and get by with less. It's part of their eccentricity. Taurean Tigers want to be expansive without being expensive.

You will not regret befriending a Taurus/Tiger. They are easy to get along with because they find it less complicated to let others know their limits from the start than to suffer unpleasant surprises later. If they don't want your screaming kid in their house, they are most likely to tell you in a nice way that little Shelly is simply impossible. No hard feelings.

Another Taurus/Tiger trait is courage. These people have the grit of a foot soldier and the mind of a Roman general. Like good, hearty red wines, they travel well, age impeccably and enhance just about any activity you can dream up.

Love

The brand of burning passion with which Taurus/Tigers are gifted from birth makes love look like a word to describe apathy. Tigers born in Taurus really fall in love. They find someone to whom they give everything, follow everywhere, involve themselves with selflessly and with an uncommon ardor, defending that person down to the very last bullet in their gun belts. Trouble is, if anything should happen to said person or a cloud settle over the relationship, Taurus/Tiger can slip into a yellow-and-black-striped despair out of which it is mightily tough to dislodge him. When the love is gone, an integral part of the Taurus/Tiger leaves with it.

In order to love one of these singular souls, you need nor really do any more than be. The Taurean Tiger figures it's up to him or her to do the adoring. "You just sit there while I go get us some drinks." Taurean Tigers like to care for others in a metaphysical or mental way. I wouldn't put my daily diet into their hands—you might be condemned to eating only beans or tomato soup. Taurus/Tiger is not fussy about variety or gourmet preparations. One must eat to live and not live to eat, is his motto. So don't fuss. And don't worry about whether your Taurus/Tiger is comfy or happy or worried—he'll let you know of his own accord. These subjects do not shy from expressing themselves.

Compatibilities

Cancer, Virgo and Capricorn appeal to your earthly side. In their ranks you're best off with Dragons, Dogs or Horses. A flight-of-fancy love life might include the watery Pisces born in Dragon or Dog years. Scorpios are not to be excluded either, particularly those of the Dog variety. Don't bother with Scorpio/Monkeys or Snakes, though, and refrain from Leo and Aquarius/Snake, Ox and even the mellow Monkey. But be your own person first. And in choosing a mate, remember to retreat from the headlong lickety split types. Seek wiser souls than you.

Home and Family

The home life of a Taurus/Tiger is not exactly paradise. Why is it so turbulent? So changeable? So fraught?

I think it might have something to do with the combination of Tigerish hotheadedness and Taurean stubbornness. Taurus/Tigers like things their own way, remember? Now, we all know that happy households depend greatly on compromise, give and take, mutability and shifting of sights. None of the above appeals to the feisty Taurus/Tiger. He plans to have his home as he sees fit. My way or the highway time.

As a parent this person will try very hard to be fair and never to mete out punishments unless no other reasonable solution has worked. Taurean Tigers are serious about their duties and want to make certain their kids achieve and behave. But sometimes their own rather unusual lives and destinies carry them far away across many lands and into fierce and exciting places. The children may be left to manage quite on their own. As everyone knows, a kid on its own can be good or can be a disaster. That's about what happens to Taurus/Tiger's kids. All or nothing.

The Taurus/Tiger child will be eccentric and self-propelled. He should be fun and like the family group as long as he is young and still dependent. As he grows older he will pull at the reins and insist on more independence than one normally wants to accord a child. Let him go. He has bigger fish to fry than a mere parent can imagine.

Profession

This person's creativity lies in his individuality. He doesn't like to think according to someone else's plan. He wants to jump in and find out for himself (even if it hurts) if the fire is really hot.

Employing such a freaky person is not very restful. Yet, the Tiger/Taurus's talents may be worth the few problems you will have getting him or her to adapt to rules and settling into routines. Once convinced that his purpose here in said office or home or shop or restaurant and brings good to the order, the Taurean Tiger will see each task through with remarkable sagacity and fervor. Of course Taurean Tigers prefer to be boss. They like to exert their gentle authority and even quite enjoy collecting the shekels that go with being a part of management. Mind you, they don't really intrinsically care about the damned money. But if it comes with the territory, so much the better.

Some jobs suitable to the Taurus/Tiger: missionary, writer, policeman (Interpol), general, political adviser, journalist, ruler.

Famous Taureans born Tiger: Robespierre, Karl Marx, Ho Chi Minh, Romain Gary, Elizabeth II, Fernand Raynaud, James Monroe, Jay Leno, Marina Vlady, Martin Gray, Penelope Cruz, Peter Frampton, Stevie Wonder.

TAURUS

ARDOR	LANGUOR
DETERMINATION	PREJUDICE
INDUSTRY	INTRACTABILITY
PATIENCE	GLUTTONY
LOGIC	COMPLACENCY
SENSUALITY	JEALOUSY

"I have"

Earth, Venus, Fixed

CAT / RABBIT

TACT	SECRETIVENESS
FINESSE	SQUEAMISHNESS
VIRTUE	PEDANTRY
PRUDENCE	DILETTANTISM
LONGEVITY	HYPOCHONDRIA
AMBITION	COMPLEXITY

"I retreat"

Negative Wood, Yin

Security-oriented and vulnerable, this is a risky combination. The Taurean born Cat requires safety and pledges and assurances and guarantees in all aspects of his life. He cannot function properly if the rent isn't paid and the kids don't all have new shoes. Taurus/Cat is not, by any stretch of the imagination, a bohemian.

While we are on the subject of imagination, let's remember that Taurus/Cats receive a lion's share of that commodity at birth. They are first inventors, innovators and breakthrough thinkers on subjects both artistic and creative. They seek their fortunes by means of their vision and inspiration. Frequently, they succeed.

Taurus/Cats are settlers. Once the fire is in the hearth and their feet are on the fender, you'll have a hell of a time wrenching one of these people loose to take in a movie or drive a few hundred miles for a beer. Taurus born Cat likes to stay at home. They are nesters and snugglers and careful collectors.

The risky business about which I spoke earlier usually arises in the life of Taurean Cats after they have arrived at some of their lofty goals. You see, success is like anything else that appears all good on the surface. We hear "success" and we think, "Ah, comfort! Ah, money! Ah, popularity!" And it's true. Yet, as all coins have a reverse side, so too does success.

If you have made it, then you can't call your life your own any longer. If your records are a hit and it looks as if you're making a mint, the taxman may come and stay for three months in your very own home! People write to you asking you to send them a lock of your hair, one of your baby teeth, and on and on.

Taurus/Cats abhor indiscriminate mingling. They enjoy having a few close acquaintances or friends in for dinner. But they don't really love having crowds surrounding their bathtubs while they bathe. So, as they are artistic people and frequently seek success with the public, these folks have quite a problem.

What has been known to occur with the ragingly successful Taurus/Cat is that once he has made it and tasted the fruits of real success, he contentedly sinks into obscurity, goes back to sitting by the fire and stays there forever. He's not a comeback person at all. He's been there. He's seen and he's conquered. That will be quite enough, thank you.

The Taurean Cat is easily hurt. It's hard for this creature to put up with the rotten world in which we all live. He doesn't hanker after rococo schemes or conjure up secret strategies. Business sharks or gangsterish types grate on the Taurus/Cat's tender nervous system and make him feel that the world is a desperate and dangerous place. He may hole up forever in a tiny town next to nowhere if only so he never has to rub elbows with lowlifes again. Taurus/Cat is a peace and love sign.

Love

A gracious and refined Taurus and a stubborn and sensuous Cat, this person will prefer uncomplicated love affairs to baroque and complex affairs of the heart. Taurus/Cats don't enjoy suffering and are not given to self-pity or sniveling. They adhere rather to the charming and comforting in love relationships.

If you love a Taurean Cat, don't provoke him or her or nag about details. The Taurus/Cat generally looks after details in his own fashion and in his own time. If you can adjust to the routines of your Taurean Cat, move ahead at the pace he or she has chosen, you'll be a lot happier for it.

Taurus/Cats are generous and expansive while on the way up. But don't be fooled into thinking this is their true nature. They are given to long spells of silence and they require calm in which to ponder their flowers growing. It is not exactly Disneyland to live with such a person. If you want somebody to tell you funny stories, there's always "Dial-a-Joke" or "Jokes.com".

Compatibilities

For you I would advise seeking partners in Capricorn or Cancer among Goats, Dogs or Pigs. You may be enticed by the self-similarity of a Virgo/Cat, down - to-earth like you yet more analytical. Pisces/Goats and Pigs make fine mates for Taureans born Cat. But don't be seduced by dashing Leos, Scorpios or Aquarians born in Rooster or Tiger. Scorpio/Rats will overpower you, too, not to mention the disastrous combination of yourself and the Scorpio/ Dragon. Ugh.

Home and Family

The decor is always splendid, cozy, warm, pleasant and welcoming around a Taurus/Cat's home. Luxury will be omnipresent but it will not show itself through the unbecoming appearance of golden angel sconces or showy, melt-down sterling silver firedogs. Subtle grace and inherent good taste will sing forth from all the furniture and objects about the place. Culturally acceptable magazines like National Geographic and Architectural Digest probably figure among the Taurus/Cat's favorite coffee table literature.

Taurean Cats tend to retreat in the face of violence. The Bull is normally a combative type. But Cats are so invariably squeamish that the Bull's heavy belligerence can never temper it enough. As a result, the Taurus/Cat will be the sort of parent or sibling who explains each interdiction, reasons with family members endlessly about why we have to do this because it's the way civilized people do this and why we cannot possibly allow ourselves to be seen doing that because it's not attractive or graceful or pleasant.

If yon have a Taurus child born Cat, turn the classical music up louder and buy a harpsichord kit. These children adore music. They love to dream. They are happiest in peaceful and pastoral surroundings. They are not fighters. You won't get anywhere with them by strict disciplinary tactics. Sit them down quietly and explain. Otherwise you might mar their gentle little psyches forever.

Profession

The work life of a Taurus/Cat person is often characterized by a swift and impressive upward swing when the person is between twenty-five and forty. These years are the ones in which the Taurus/Cat can still believe and has not yet been hurt or disappointed or discouraged by the roiling big bad world.

After the age of forty or forty-five, this person may seem to have run plum out of gas. This slowdown is the result of two important factors in the life of a Taurus/Cat. First, he's been disappointed and has shrugged off too many sullying experiences and wants an end to it. Secondly, because he is careful and cautious with spending and saving, he can afford to sit back and relax away from the madding crowd he hates so fervently.

As a boss, this person is respectable and even a bit sanctimonious at times, with his eternal good examples. As an employee this subject is almost a saint. He won't want to stay late at the office much, as his home beckons more strongly than money or advancement. But he will be both industrious and dutiful.

Taurus/Cat should choose from artistic or glamour careers for the most success: set designer, singer, actor, cabinetmaker, piano tuner, diplomat, landscape architect, jeweler, potter, inventor.

Some famous Taurus/Cats: Orson Welles, Dr. Benjamin Spock, Judy Collins, Christopher Cross, Dale Earnhardt, Dule Hill, Enrique Iglesias, Harvey Keitel, Jacques Lanzmann, José Arthur, Jean-Paul Belmondo, Robert Zemeckis, Tony Danza.

TAURUS

ARDOR	LANGUOR
DETERMINATION	PREJUDICE
INDUSTRY	INTRACTABILITY
PATIENCE	GLUTTONY
LOGIC	COMPLACENCY
SENSUALITY	JEALOUSY

"I have"

Earth, Venus, Fixed

DRAGON

STRENGTH	RIGIDITY
SUCCESS	MISTRUST
GOOD HEALTH	DISSATISFACTION
ENTHUSIASM	INFATUATION
PLUCK	BRAGGADOCIO
SENTIMENTALITY	VOLUBILITY

"I preside"

Positive Wood, Yang

Might and bite come together here, giving us a powerhouse of brutal energy and excessive adroitness. Nobody will ever tell you that they "just couldn't care less" about a Taurus/Dragon. People either adore Taurus Dragons or they detest them!

Wood and earth. Two organic elements. On the one hand, this native exudes down-to the-ground good sense, but on the other he is tempestuously foolish and selfishly attention-getting. Taurus and Dragon form an unforgettable couple.

Strong opinions characterize people born under this pair of signs. "I should think" or "I would suppose" is here replaced by "It is!" and "You're wrong!" and "Two and two are not four!" and "That's that!"

This person is competent. At an early age he will head out of the nest, forage around the world in a thousand different jobs, pursuits and causes. Then, just when you think he's about to become a bona fide lifetime failure, Taurus/Dragon gets it together, comes back to his home town, is instantly hired in the top job in the business of his or her choice, and within two years he has been promoted to president.

The Taurus/Dragon is haughty. He blusters, "Why should I apply myself until I am good and ready?" Conceited? Yes. But the thing is, people born under these two signs generally end up getting what they want. They are so blatantly determined and industrious (and moreover are not shy about admitting it) that others can't help it. They are impressed.

Taurus/Dragons are plucky. When you meet one you'll see what I mean. They've always done things nobody else has tried, like running off to a foreign country where a revolution is going on or dancing topless in a bikini on a bistro table in Saudi Arabia where even the female dogs and cats wear veils. Taurus/Dragons are daring to a fault.

It is not uncommon for the Taurus/Dragon's travels and derring-do to be financed by somebody more settled than he—an ex-spouse or a parent or even just an old friend. Scruples are not a Taurus/Dragon affliction. So long as the money keeps rolling, he or she does not care where it comes from. As far as the Taurus/Dragon is concerned, his own immediate cause surpasses in value all others. When he's tired of it, when he's had it with helping starving Bedouins and wants to take a break, Taurus/Dragon might rush out and spend his last dinar on a bunch of new clothes. Then, he quickly telegraphs home to Kalamazoo for airfare.

There is a kind of mute force present in the Taurus/Dragon's nature. Rather than being the exclusively vocal fire breather most Dragons are, this Dragon tends for the most part to seem quiet. Except, of course, if provoked. And being of such strong and unshakable opinions, Taurus/Dragons are always provoked. "What do you mean by that?" seems a harmless question, doesn't it? Well, try asking it of a Taurus/Dragon sometime. Then stand back. Horns and scales quiver, a roaring sound emanates from the chest, then— thar she blows! You would do well to remain seated or the enraged Taurus/Dragon will blow you over with his hot shower of protestations.

It's a bit off-putting, I admit. Taurus/Dragons cannot really know everything. Yet, no matter what we do to counter them, they go on believing that what they think and do is right and proper and the best. Taurus/Dragons love a good fight. When they storm the Bastille of your defenses, they are not only defending their cherished ideas, Taurus/Dragons are cruising for a good old-fashioned row. They'll throw themselves into a scrap with more verve than practically any other sign. No blind rages either. Low blows and hair-pulling allowed.

Love

Of course this Taurus born in a Dragon year is most sentimental. No matter how pushy and aggressive this person seems, if you scratch the surface you'll discover a substance not unlike swan's down, in great quantity. Taurus/Dragons are serious lovers. They admire and adulate their mates. Once they have found the person they will love for a long, long time, Taurus/Dragons are capable of remaining utterly faithful to said mate.

The Dragon is interested in love and in having romance in his life. But I'd venture he is actually more interested in his own advancement in the world. In other words, Taurus/Dragons are not known for their grandiose, torrid extramarital love affairs. But they are often known for their jealousy and excessive need for attention from lovers and mistresses.

I know a Taurus/Dragon lady who repeatedly kept her lover up all night "discussing" their relationship. Not long ago, she boasted to me of a trick she once played on him after a night-long row. "At six a.m., he just turned over and went to sleep on me," she explained. "He always gets up at seven to go to work."

"He must have been very tired," I opined. Poor guy needed at least ne hour's sleep.

"So do you know what I did?" said the Dragon lady. "I went in the kitchen and got a rope. And I tied all four doors in his bedroom together by their handles. Then I brought the rope over and lashed his sleeping form to his bed."

Aghast, I asked her how she could do such a terrible thing to someone she loved,

"I wanted to talk some more. I knew that if I didn't tie him down as soon as he woke up he'd leave. Then, I jumped on the bed and shook him awake," she told me with a twinkly smile of pride.

"What happened then?" I was very curious by now.

"He talked to me," she declared, as though there was no other solution. "I didn't let him go to work until eleven-thirty."

And they're still together. Isn't that amazing?

Compatibilities

The beautiful trouble with Dragons is that they get along with hordes of other signs, other tough Taurean Dragons not excepted. You will find possibles among Cancer, Virgo and Capricorn/Rat and Monkey subjects. You will also be turned on for life by the sleek Virgo born in Snake. You won't have any trouble cohabiting with Pisces/Roosters, Rats or Monkeys. If I were you, though, I'd give Leo and Scorpio/Oxen and Dogs the slip. You need to preserve all your fight for your own advancement. Don't mingle intimacy with friendship where Aquarius/Oxen and Dogs are concerned, either.

Home and Family

Despite his penchant for globetrotting and excitement, the Taurus/Dragon usually makes an excellent parent. His family preoccupies him no little and he wants them to love, honor and obey him. In return, he provides well, bringing home plenty of bacon for the gang.

Remember, this person is a Dragon. And Dragon is the most secretly affectionate of Chinese animal signs. Emotional attachments stir this subject deeply. Taurus/Dragon will take every move his or her child makes personally. If the kid gets good marks, then Taurus/Dragon pats himself on the back and thinks, "My child is a genius." (Accent on the my.) Or conversely, if the Taurean Dragon's son is a juvenile delinquent who robs banks, the parent will take it badly, feel personally responsible and not spare the rod.

The Taurus/Dragon child will be boisterous. The need for attention that comes with the Taurus/Dragon territory may shock an unsuspecting parent. The child must be channeled early on into activities that require the energy to be applied. Positive behavior must be encouraged. This child's parent will often be weary from applauding. A Dragon born in Taurus is a uniquely talented performer. Let this child follow his instincts. If you don't, he will follow them anyway.

Profession

Taurus/Dragons are both overachievers and malcontents. No matter whether they take up whether it's social work or sculpture, teaching or medicine, these subjects are Hell-bent to succeed. They often rise to the top of the ladder. They make testy employees whose aim it is to take over the store. On their way to the best position in the company, they may whine a lot: The water cooler is too far from their desk. Or the sun shines in their window at the wrong time of day. Or maybe the salary is too low or the working conditions too rigorous. Whatever their job, Taurus/Dragons air their grievances—abundantly. Nobody can ever expect to really get along with a Taurus/Dragon in work situations. Instead, they put up with him, admire and revere him. Taurean Dragons won't have it any other way.

Ideal professions for the Taurus born Dragon are: Advertising executive, artist (all kinds), athlete, movie star, radio or TV personality, psychiatrist, college professor.

Who's who in Taurus/Dragonland: Salvador Dali, Sigmund Freud, Jean Gabin, Shirley Temple, Yehudi Menuhin, Al Pacino, Burt Young, Charles Aznavour, Edouard Molinaro, Hosni Mubarak (Egypt), James L. Brooks, Jennifer Capriati, Johannes Brahms, Lee Majors, Peter Benchley, Renaud, Rick Nelson, Stan Mikita, Yannick Noah.

TAURUS

ARDOR	LANGUOR
DETERMINATION	PREJUDICE
INDUSTRY	INTRACTABILITY
PATIENCE	GLUTTONY
LOGIC	COMPLACENCY
SENSUALITY	JEALOUSY

"I have"

Earth, Venus, Fixed

SNAKE

INTUITION	DISSIMULATION
ATTRACTIVENESS	EXTRAVAGANCE
DISCRETION	LAZINESS
SAGACITY	CUPIDITY
CLAIRVOYANCE	PRESUMPTION
COMPASSION	EXCLUSIVENESS

"I sense"

Negative, Fire, Yang

This is the most natural of Snakes. As Snake people often display cosmic leanings and cleave to the other worldly, the presence of Taurus grounds them. This Snake will be intuitive as usual, and wonderfully discreet. But the Taurus part of the character will lend earthiness.

There is a definite talent here for acquisition. Snakes like money and often come by it with more ease than others. They covet luxury, too, and revel in comfort. The Taurus is similar in that what he gets, he keeps.

Art and beauty hold much for the Taurean Snake. He not only wants to participate in its creation (and he might very well); the Taurus/Snake wants to bathe in a totally artistic ambience. The Taurus/Snake's sense of luxury is not like, say, the Pig's desire for live-in opulence and gluttonous wealth. Taurean Snakes are more drawn to serious beauty than they are to ostentatious display.

Like all natives of the Snake sign, the Taurus/Snake will spend his life in full battle with his archenemy: laziness. As Taureans frequently suffer from languorousness, are stubborn and sometimes eat rather too much, imagine what the Snake's lassitude can wreak on this person's waistline.

Like all Snakes, this native will possess a special brand of beauty. Snakes are always wonderful to look at. But Taurean Snakes have added solidity and will be less translucent and coldly gorgeous than other Snakes.

This Taurean will be a procrastinator. He or she will start and stop the same task a hundred times before finally completing it down to the last detail. It's not that Taurean Snakes are hesitant or lack self-confidence. But this person wants to take his time about getting to the end of everything—from love-making to basket weaving. He's not a plodder. He's a "fit and starter."

People born in Snake years under the sign of Taurus appear straight-faced. They strike one as a mite too serious. But surprisingly, the Taurean Snake character is capable of gigantic feats of silliness. I know one Taurus/Snake woman who regularly causes a dinner party of six or eight guests to collapse in a helpless heap of laughter by her zany antics. It is a common miscal-cula-tion to find these subjects forbidding.

Dissimulation is always a problem for Snakes. The Taurus logic and true patience may temper this bad habit but it will still surface from time to time anyway. Snakes tell fibs—even to themselves. It may even be part of the reason they operate slowly when confronted with inevitable conflict. They are capable of telling themselves that whatever is happening is not really hap-pening at all.

Jealousy will crop up here, too. Taureans are jealous beasts. Snakes have a hard time with faithfulness. The very combination presents obvious problems. Why do I stay with Jack? Because Jack is mine. Why do I cheat on Jack? Because I love to seduce. Why do I go back to Jack? Because Jack is mine.

Love

As a lover or mate this person will be so attractive that you will want to spoil him or her to death. My advice? Don't. The Taurean Snake will take care of that on his or her own. Fact is, natives of Snake and Taurus both need to have a structure in their lives in order to accomplish anything. If you love one of these characters, help put some starch in his sails. Bring some order into the kitchen, and sharpen those tools she left lying out in the rain. Hang up the clothes you find scattered everywhere, and lay down the law about self-discipline. It's the biggest favor you can do for this slightly indolent, slip-pery character.

In turn, the Taurean Snake will hold you in high regard, listen to your woes and give sound advice on all of your problems, keep the larder and the library filled with exciting exotica and, in short, seduce you anew every day.

Compatibilities

Normally you get along with Cancer, Virgo, Capricorn and Pisces in the form of Oxen, Dragons and Roosters. You need stability but are magnetized by folly. Watch out for headstrong Leo/Tigers and Pigs. And don't get caught up in either Scorpio or Aquarius/Tiger's catchy refrains. Keep your cool in the face of these enchanters or the result could be disastrous.

Home and Family

For this person surroundings are ultra-important. She will want to call in the finest decorators and finish the bedroom doors in Chinese red lacquer. He will insist on creamy leather couches and tufted armchairs from England. These souls are the epitome of plush. Theirs will be a home in which you can flop in style.

Security means a great deal to this person's ultimate happiness. A family may not be quick in coming (procrastination rears its head) but when it does, the Taurus/Snake will not make light of it. As a parent, Taurus/Snake is generally reliable and sensible as well as sensitive.

The child Taurus/Snake should be nurtured and never pushed. He or she will react badly to any attempt by aggressive parents to steer a course he or she has not chosen personally. Taurus/Snake kids will have a silly streak that can be fun, but then again it might not always amuse the parents to have a clown around the dinner table. Taurus/Snake may be a rather taciturn child, keeping much to himself, taking solitary walks and knowing how to play alone in his room. Do not jolt.

Profession

Taking risks is not this subject's forte. He is serious about gain and not one to fritter or gamble money. As a result, you will usually find Taurus/Snake in surefire professions where earning power is high and the promise of retirement in the not-too-distant future certain. His talents lie in intellectual areas or in the classical professions.

As a boss, the Taurus/Snake may not be too terrific because he is slow about making decisions. Taurean Snakes are not adept at delegating authority, preferring to keep most of it for themselves and only issuing permits to those they deem worthy. But as an employee, providing he is well remunerated and his occasional pranks don't get in the way of progress, the Taurean Snake might make a handsome and useful addition to any work environment.

Jobs that might suit the Taurus/Snake personality are: professor, artist, librarian, lawyer, doctor, and all other classical professions right on down through to pharmacist. Then too, these people make excellent designers, stunning performers and remarkable precision engineers.

Some famous Taurus/Snakes: Henry Fonda, I.M. Pei, Audrey Hepburn, Danièle Darrieux, Nora Ephron, Paavo Tapio Lipponen (Finland), Richie Valens.

TAURUS

HORSE

TAURUS		HORSE	
ARDOR	LANGUOR	PERSUASIVENESS	SELFISHNESS
DETERMINATION	PREJUDICE	UNSCRUPULOUSNESS	AUTONOMY
INDUSTRY	INTRACTABILITY	POPULARITY	REBELLION
PATIENCE	GLUTTONY	STYLE	HASTE
LOGIC	COMPLACENCY	DEXTERITY	ANXIETY
SENSUALITY	JEALOUSY	ACCOMPLISHMENT	PRAGMATISM

"I have"

Earth, Venus, Fixed

"I demand"

Positive Fire, Yang

Greedy for dominion over others, the Taurus/Horse wants to play the beau rôle in all of life's dramas. The Horse is a prancer and even when housed in the mind and body of the drudge-tolerant Taurus, that old pony will kick up his heels, show who's boss and even occasionally throw his rider—just to keep the record straight.

There is frequently much talent apparent early in the life of Taurean Horses. They may be prodigies in music or art or even in sports or intellectual pursuits. I wouldn't be surprised if those kids who win international competitions at age six include many Taurus/Horses among them. The Taurus/Horse child's personality is obedient and well-behaved, diligent and ambitious in the first part of his life. Parental urging is heeded by the Taurean born Horse child. This kid practices his piano.

But somewhere in the melee of adolescence, when the first interminglings with peers begins, the genius in Taurean Horses becomes compromised by social life, by the demands of a "normal" existence. Not that the clever Taurean Horse can ever really fit in. He cannot. He is different, separate by virtue of both his specialness and his bitterness at not being chosen for a Nobel Prize at age thirteen. Taurus/Horses find satisfaction in greatness. Otherwise they are grumpy because nobody recognizes how brilliant they really are.

Growing up is a comedown to a lot of Taurean Horses. It was great when Mom and Pop applauded every breath and your fifth-grade teacher told you that you had natural gifts unlike any she'd ever seen. But being an adult is a terrible drag. You have to go out there and prove yourself, fight your way among people far less talented than yourself who, by some fluke, advance more quickly than you do.

So let me give you some advice, Taurus/Horse. It's true that you surely have more talent and ability than most. You are a marvelous human being. But you are socially lazy. You don't want to make that extra effort to ring up somebody who needs a smile, to go call on the sick grandmother or the guy who said he'd give you a contract. You don't want mere action. You want privileges. And I'm sorry to break this to you, Taurus/Horse, but privilege evolves from the whole experience of getting to the top. If you back out before you begin it won't happen for you for long. There will always be some less talented, more humble or wily person who comes along and pulls the magic carpet out from under you.

Nobody can say that Taurus/Horses are not conscientious workers. They are always the first ones at the office and the last to go home at night. Taurus/Horses are materialistic and love to own beautiful things. They tend to show off their wealth and dress in rather colorful yet conservative clothes. They are far from dull. They have plenty to talk about. Taurean Horses are responsible and respectable people. They grow more discreet and have better manners as they get older and move away from the childish self-image of prodigy who can do anything and get away with it because of superlative talent.

Actually, the Taurus/Horse, with all the brilliance given him at birth, is more of an instinctive being than he is an intellectual. He can think but he would rather operate on hunches. He can reflect but he'd rather play music—or even baseball! This person needs much understanding from his entourage—patience, good humor and solicitude.

Love

How, you may ask, can this egomaniacal demigenius stop preening long enough to love anyone? Well, the fact is that love is the only area in which the Taurus/Horse does not deem him- or herself automatically superior. Taurean Horses are excessively susceptible to love affairs. They are capable of giving up everything for the sake of gaining the affections of the person in their lives. Taurus/Horse people care enormously about their public image and worry about what others think of them. Therefore, discretion is an important factor in the Taurus/Horse's love life. He doesn't particularly enjoy bandying his romantic business around. He or she will hardly be the type to hold hands or kiss in public.

The Taurus/Horse needs someone in his or her life who is willing to hover in the wings while he or she performs. I don't, however, recommend anyone too long-suffering and self-sacrificial. The Taurus/Horse doesn't want to be fawned over. Usually he or she has had enough of that in youth.

So give your Taurean Horse a challenge. Tempt him or her to come off his self-imposed pedestal. Drag your Taurus/Horse victim to parties and get him involved in social work. Otherwise he may turn into a stay-at-home misanthrope who feels misunderstood and complains a lot. Taurean Horses need to be jollied up, tickled and taught to laugh—especially at themselves.

Compatibilities

You'll get on with Cancer, Virgo and Capricorn/Tigers, Roosters and Goats. You'll feel superior to them in one way, yet they know how to stand up to your sometimes magnified self-image. Pisces/Tigers confront well, too, so you may find yourself entrapped by one. But the Pisces/Goat is the one you would really die to catch. Good luck. Rats, above all of the Scorpio and Aquarian families will not do. Make yourself scarce for Leo/Monkeys, Aquarius/Oxen and Pigs, and give Scorpio/Pigs a pass, too.

Home and Family

The Taurean Horse's home will be his castle. No place is better suited to his temperament and no place on the outside makes him feel comfortable. In fact, I would venture that all Taureans born in Horse years are at their very best in their own very personal surroundings.

As a parent, the Taurean Horse may at first be thrown off guard by his children's innocence. He wonders, "What do these little people really want from me?" Nothing but love? How terrific! A family life of their very own is the best way for Taurus/Horses to take their minds off themselves.

As a child, the Taurean Horse will be almost too good to be true. You will be amazed at his abilities and want to send him to Hollywood or Harvard. You will find this little person's behavior exemplary and you will love the little darling to pieces. One word of advice: Take it easy on the kid! Don't push too hard, and keep the applause to a minimum or his head will grow too big for his social life. Encourage his talents but don't forget to prepare him for the real world.

Profession

Sometimes, of course, the Taurean Horse is so gifted that he begins an artistic or art-related career very young and sticks to it. But we know that in the lives of kids who start out very early, there is many a slip 'twixt the high school stage and the Oscar. The wise Taurean Horse goes to university or pursues some kind of practical studies parallel to his creative pursuit. He makes a very demanding boss. As an employee, the Taurus/Horse is generally much appreciated by superiors fur his rigorous attention to detail and his real desire for advancement.

Taurean Horse can choose almost any artistic career if they can take the heat that goes with it. Otherwise there are many art-related fields such as production or communications. And why not law? Or advertising? All areas where one needs practicality and poise will do.

Some famous Taurus/Horses: Ulysses S. Grant, Mike Wallace, Barbra Streisand, Amadeo Giannini, Ella Fitzgerald, Janet Jackson, Jasper Johns, Kurt Godel, Laetitia Casta, Martha Graham, Pat Summerall, Paul Mazursky, Pennel Roberts, Vladimir Lenin.

TAURUS

GOAT

ARDOR	LANGUOR	INVENTION	PARASITISM
DETERMINATION	PREJUDICE	LACK OF FORESIGHT	SENSITIVITY
INDUSTRY	INTRACTABILITY	PERSEVERANCE	TARDINESS
PATIENCE	GLUTTONY	WHIMSY	PESSIMISM
LOGIC	COMPLACENCY	GOOD MANNERS	TASTE
SENSUALITY	JEALOUSY	IMPRACTICALITY	WORRY

"I have"

Earth, Venus, Fixed

"I depend"

Negative Fire, Yang

This person is, by turns, a taciturn pixie, an industrious nitwit and a brilliant dreamer. Great genius often visits people born Taurus/Goat. And, if properly handled, this inner spark or enormous creative ability can take them far in both worldly and personal development. But without optimum growing conditions, this subject will spend his or her life seeming to putter about, half-finishing projects and partly realizing dreams.

Essentially, the Taurus/Goat struggles his whole life long with a yearning for security that comes from without. The Taurus character is slow but solid—even stodgy at times. Taureans are down-to-earth, acquisitive and sensual. Taurus likes order and thrives on certain sameness that others might deem monotony. But the Goat nature is evanescent, shifting and spasmodic. Goats excel by fits and starts.

Visualize the nimble mountain goat propelled by a fierce effort up a steep incline. A great impressive leap gets the Goat sure-footedly to an inaccessible peak. Here comes Taurus. And what does Taurus do to the flighty Goat? He causes him to sit down, look around, examine a few of the wild flowers underfoot, admire himself in a nearby pool and even set up camp on that peak until some new impetus comes along to force his next gigantic push.

Taurus and Goat are complementary signs. Slowness and sure-footedness work well together. So do logic and invention. Patience goes well with perseverance. There are parts of this character that assure us a totally calm human being. And most Taurus/Goats do possess composure.

Behind the scenes, however, we find determination opposed to lack of foresight, languor as against intractability. These contrary traits are constantly at battle. Repeatedly, for concrete earthly reasons to be sure, Taurus/Goat's spirit is invaded by his inner contradictions. This makes him by turns pessimistic and anxious. The personality develops flaws of near Mephistophelian proportions.

How does all of this apply to the Taurus/Goat's daily life? Well, I've known my share of Taureans born in Goat years. And they all give in to periods of self-doubt, frustration and even violence.

Taurus/Goats are viscerally attracted to what is beautiful. They have more discerning good taste in one hoof than you or I have in our whole bodies. Normally the Taurus/Goat builds, creates, invents, interprets and decorates. And, when not actively engaged in said activities, this person backs off from society, takes refuge in pastoral surroundings and plots his next stroke of genius.

The iffy part or this portrait only arises when Taurus/Goats are hindered from implementing their brilliant moves. Financial considerations bore Taurus/Goats. They are usually nigh unto incapable of turning their creations into ready cash. They lack drive and they anger easily when pushed. If anybody, and I mean anybody, should so much as dare to cast a shadow on their parade, Taurus/Goats surrender. Then, they seethe. They don't give up. Their dreams are still intact. But the interfering party, he who hurls the wrench into Taurus/Goat's works, will not go unpunished. Revenge – even violence—is not out of the question.

Taurus/Goats cannot discuss their frustrations. They are not the whimpering "feel sorry for me" type. And they aren't excessively articulate either. So, Taurus/Goats are either peaceful or else they are out there swinging. They have their own timetables and their own personal aesthetic. Don't get in the way of either and the Taurus/Goat will be happy to spend the rest of his/her life eating off your plate.

Love

To hear jilted Taurus/Goats talk you would think all of their various "exes" (wives, husbands, companions) were but a pack of thieves, strumpets and pimps. Taurus/Goat likes to be loved—and cared for. He needs enormous security and is not very apt at providing same. He also needs praise. But he can't give very much of that either. Taurean Goats simply have to be loved for the part-time jollies they can give. They have little staying power in love. They fly off the handle at the slightest forgotten birthday or wedding anniversary. They attach importance to roses and Valentines, but they might just forget your cat in the refrigerator overnight. For serious mates, Taurus/Goats are exasperating.

And Taurus/Goats need serious mates. They cannot function in a couple where they have to wear the trousers, bring home the bacon or bathe the baby. Taurus/Goats can—and only just—create. They have no sense of time, no memory for anything more important than their mate's credit card numbers and they refuse to see the reason to change.

If you are prepared to be strong and tough and police the everyday life of some adorable but violent and wacky artiste, run out and lasso yourself a Taurus/Goat. I'm sure there are lots of them going to waste. Taurus/Goat is an inertia worshiper. Yours is probably just sitting there prettily, waiting to be discovered in a long-defunct Hollywood drugstore.

Compatibilities

You'll like Pisces/Pigs and Horses. You'll be charmed by Virgo/Cats, and entranced by the cultivated Virgo/Pig. Capricorns and Cancers, both Monkeys and Horses, will please you, too. Your best bet is found among Capricorn/Monkeys, but they are very much in demand so you will need to hurry. Don't take up with Leo/Oxen or Dogs. Keep your distance from Scorpio/Tigers and Oxen and run when you see an Aquarius in a Dog or a Tiger costume.

Home and Family

The home situation is dependent upon whom Taurus/Goat can depend. If the family unit is solid and the central pivotal force provides a fertile and comfortable ambience for the subject to evolve in, Taurus/Goat will make a delightfully blissful parent.

Taurean Goats love to play, to gambol hither and yon over hilt and dale, to frolic with their children and show them how to appreciate life's finer things. Yon may find Taurus/Goat in the basement fashioning a slick new toy for the baby or in the kitchen frosting cupcakes with perfect little faces, each different and each precisely the likeness of a family member.

Of course, you must also expect that the toy may not be finished until baby is of voting age and those cupcakes may be stale by the time all the expert facial decorations are complete. Somebody has got to push this Goat up those basement stairs, or out of the kitchen and into the dining room with the dessert. Whenever you meet up with this character, look for the person holding the cattle prod just inches away.

As children, Taurus/Goats must be patiently encouraged to pick up toys, to complete homework projects, to follow through on tennis serves, to check the temperature before going out in a frigid world wearing only a T-shirt. A careful parent is in order. This child will of course be charming and a wizard with his hands. This talented kid needs discipline, a firm but loving hand that slowly, imperceptibly loosens the rope that tethers the child to home. There is probably a form of genius here. But it will remain a lazy prisoner if left un-nurtured.

Taurus/Goats are perfect grist for the mills of stage mothers the world over. But I wouldn't count too heavily on this person's professional orientation taking him or her much further than the front door. Unless—and this is crucial—others who have noted the genius are willing to sacrifice their own notoriety, give up their own personal ambition for the sake of their prodigy's success.

Profession

The advice I can give to Taurus/Goats is slim. I don't pretend to know how to alter this person's tendency to indolence without using force. I am, as you know by now, of the Sherman tank school of human dynamics. "If you don't feel like doing something, do it anyway," is my motto. This theory doesn't work with Taurus/Goats. What does work? Maybe lots of affection, warmth, coziness and endurance, encouragement and blind unquestioning faith in Taurus/Goat's work. I'd say that Taurus/Goats who spy that mountain peak from way far away at age fifteen or less and consciously undertake to conquer that peak by age forty are way ahead of Taurus/Goats who do not find their challenge early. Taurus/Goats must surround themselves with richness and approval, sound advisers and steel-nerved allies. Such foresight is, however, not native to the Taurus/Goat. Will somebody please give this creature a shove off the starting block?

Ideal professions for the Taurus/Goat are: Genius, movie star, artist (all kinds) and diva.

Famous Taurus/Goats. Laurence Olivier, Honoré de Balzac, Rudolph Valentino (Charm, talent, comfort and more talent). Also: Chow Tun-Fat, Eva Peron, George Goebels, Jacques Dutronc, Katharine Hepburn, Philippe Séguin, Robert Morse, Teresa Brewer, Willie Mays.

TAURUS

ARDOR	LANGUOR
DETERMINATION	PREJUDICE
INDUSTRY	INTRACTABILITY
PATIENCE	GLUTTONY
LOGIC	COMPLACENCY
SENSUALITY	JEALOUSY

"I have"

Earth, Venus, Fixed

MONKEY

猴

IMPROVISATION	DECEIT
CUNNING	RUSE
STABILITY	LOQUACITY
SELF-INVOLVEMENT	LEADERSHIP
WIT	SILLINESS
OPPORTUNISM	ZEAL

"I plan"

Positive Metal, Yin

Here is one Monkey whose ruse and trickery are satisfied to remain in the wings for a lifetime. Taurus settles the busy, agile Monkey character. This is a fortuitous combination of signs.

Taurus/Monkeys are stable. Their equilibrium sticks out all over them. Capable of emotional highs and lows like everybody else, the Taurus/Monkey sets himself apart by dealing with trauma better than most. Beset by loss or tragedy, this creature remains buoyant through it all. Of course he will be aggrieved by the death of someone near. Naturally, he will pine for the lost loved one. Certainly, the Taurus/Monkey is able to sob along with the best of us. But he will also be among the first to rise from a wet pillow, place his feet squarely on the floor and decide to design better days for himself.

I am not describing, however, the jack-in-the-box resilience or the Rooster, who never gets too involved in the first place and therefore digs himself out faster. Taurus/Monkey is, after all, Taurean. He feels things profoundly and is devoted to his emotional attachments. But Taurus/Monkeys are sensible. They know instinctively when to give in. They are not afraid to surrender and start over when no alternative presents itself. Taurus/Monkeys are savvy.

Monkeys born in Taurus will be realistic people. They are not given to vapid dreaming or empty longings for things or experiences they can never have.

Taurus/Monkeys are temperate, take their methodical time about accomplishing tasks and don't settle for slapdash results. Others to whom the Taurus/Monkey has promised favor, a ride to the PTA meeting or a loan, can count on this subject never to let them down. Taurus/Monkeys will either categorically say, "No, I can't," or "Yes I'd be glad to," with a smile. And if, for some reason beyond his control, a Taurus/Monkey cannot come across with the goods, he will simply and in due time call or write or holler to apologize.

The equilibrium of people born under this marriage of signs is their single most important virtue. When you feel all right about yourself vis-à-vis the world, nothing actually can stand in the way of your happiness. Taurus/Monkeys rarely doubt themselves. Oh, they may have private moments of panic. But you'll never see a Taurus/Monkey dragging himself along whimpering about how miserable he feels inside. Instead, he will take pains to exhibit his best side, to inspire confidence in others and rarely, if ever, to place blame for his own shortcomings on colleagues or cohorts.

The Taurus/Monkey knows his own strength. Therefore, if a noisy Leo/Dragon or pushy Aries/Ox wants the limelight, Taurus/Monkey doesn't mind sitting behind the curtain feeding the boss his lines. Taurus/Monkey leadership abilities are obvious. But he doesn't need to sit on the throne to be happy using them.

Taurean Monkeys are kind, too. They go out of their way to lend a hand, cheer up a sick friend, or jolly up a grump. But with this, despite their basic generosity of spirit, Taurus/Monkeys personify independence. They need no company for activities such as going to movies or concerts, traveling, eating, dancing, and so on. It's not that Taurus/Monkeys do not adore company. But so at one are they with their own rhythms, they don't require a second opinion or even a sounding board in order to know what they enjoy in life. So if you need a Taurus/Monkey, you can call on him for help. But when you don't write SOS in the sky or jiggle the Taurus/Monkey's chain, he may just be off by himself on a bike hike around Eastern Europe.

It seems we can find no failing in this monster of stability. Yet, people do complain about Taurus/Monkeys. What they say is that Monkeys born Taurean possess such a hearty measure of self-confidence and pep that by comparison, others may feel like just so many slouches. And it's true. The Taurus/Monkey only offends by reflection. His character is so sterling, his integrity so dear, that others feel small next to him.

Taurus/Monkeys are modest too. So we cannot even accuse them of bravado. They're bright and funny, good listeners and dexterous in the extreme.

Taurus/Monkeys are devoted and uncomplicated. But don't ever try to corner one. You won't be able to fence him in. Don't expect him to hang around and mope if rejected or disobliged. This character is all of a piece. Therein lies his unbeatable force.

Love

Faithfulness, as we all know, is relative. Everyone has a slightly different point of view and interpretation of what it means to be constant in love. To a Taurus/Monkey, faithfulness in relationships is directly connected to loyalty, friendship and dedication. This person is certainly adept at loving others. Yet, he will never get involved in any long-term love affair or marriage that threatens to compromise his autonomy. For Taurus/Monkeys, mutual respect and freedom are synonymous with love.

I have never known a Taurus/Monkey whose passion for another human being crippled him. To a Monkey born in Taurus, incapacity is death. If he feels a weakness approaching his knees and can practically hear the butterflies flapping about his stomach, the Taurus/Monkey will be gone in a wink, pleasantly and preferably without harsh words. The Taurus/Monkey is likely to want a longstanding life commitment in love. But the concessions incumbent upon such a commitment may daunt him. The prospect of long dull evenings around the glowing hearth will discourage the Taurus/Monkey from early marriage. And by time he gets around to accepting a love alliance that is sure to cramp his style, the Taurus/Monkey may consider himself too old and set in his ways to actually implement it.

There is something of the eternal child in his character. He's charming but he is also elusive. Taurus/Monkey is a footloose soul who frequently imagines himself in settled loving care. But very often he ends up like Peter Pan left behind by Wendy and the Boys to fend for himself in Never-Never Land.

Compatibilities

Normally you should be compatible with Cancer, Virgo, Capricorn and Pisces/ Dragons. Dragons and Monkeys respect each other a lot. You also get along with Rats of the Cancer, Virgo and Capricorn persuasions. I'd advise you to look into the possibility of a lifetime Pisces/Rat, too. They are sweet and strong-minded at the same time. I cannot see why you are not allowed a Scorpio/Tiger, but the odds are astrologically against longevity in such relationships. Scorpio/Snakes and Aquarius/Dragons are also forbidden territory. Forget Leo/Ox, Tiger and Horse people. They are too egocentric for you.

Home and Family

Taurus/Monkeys (if they ever get around to it) make excellent parents. They are serious and caring. Also, they have a childlike quality themselves and so are amusing and playful with their kids. And of course they always provide.

As siblings, aunts and uncles and cousins, Taureans born in Monkey years are dy- na – mite! The element of liberal movement implied in such nonpassionate relationships appeals to the Taurus/Monkey. He'll bring his nephew the most extraordinary toys and take his favorite cousins on trips to faraway places. He'll gladly offer his participation in family projects or build a new swimming pool for his little sister Sara's suburban ranch house.

In order to develop a healthy Taurus/Monkey child, parents must try to allow him freedom to evolve in his own private space. Taurus/Monkey children may go off on their own too often to please a clinging parent. They will definitely leave any suffocating family atmosphere at the earliest possible moment. To ensure this person's happiness as an adult, he must always be given choices and never be forced to struggle against excessive authority. And no matter what you do as the parents of this bubbly, capable achiever, he will soon be off into the world to seek his fortune.

Profession

Taurus/Monkeys like to spend money. They therefore usually know how to earn it. As I have already said, these people are industrious and willing to pitch in and help out in almost all situations. These traits do not hinder the Taurus/Monkey's progress in career pursuits.

Taurus/Monkeys are affable, too. They enjoy meeting new people, exchanging ideas with them and learning new methods of doing things. Sales and public relations are suitable jobs for Taurus/Monkeys, as are positions in journalism or medicine. Most important, of course, is that the career choice allow for mobility. The Taurus/Monkey may, for example make a terrific photographer. But if he is obliged to sit in a dinky office somewhere taking pictures of babies with topknots in a cold white studio, all his talent will drain out before he gets a chance to apply himself. He hates to be confined. But put this energetic photographer on location in the thickest fray of the fashion or advertising world and hear that shutter click gaily away.

Uppermost in orienting a person born in Taurus/Monkey is the acquisition of a sound liberal education. The idle Taurus/Monkey mind is never a happy one. There are few fields in which he will not excel and he is especially drawn to those that excite his curiosity. Once he has a bit of knowledge on a subject that interests him, the Taurus/Monkey can study on his own, research and assimilate for a long time without further tutelage.

Famous Taurus/Monkeys: J.M. Barrie, Leonardo da Vinci, Harry Truman, Sugar Ray Leonard, Jill Clayburgh, Pope John Paul II, Anouk Aimée, Christine Bravo, Christine Ockrent, Elvire Popesco, Michel Audiard, Pia Zadora.

The New Astrology

TAURUS

ARDOR	LANGUOR
DETERMINATION	PREJUDICE
INDUSTRY	INTRACTABILITY
PATIENCE	GLUTTONY
LOGIC	COMPLACENCY
SENSUALITY	JEALOUSY

"I have"

Earth, Venus, Fixed

ROOSTER

RESILIENCE	COCKINESS
ENTHUSIASM	BOASTFULNESS
CANDOR	BLIND FAITH
CONSERVATISM	PEDANTRY
CHIC	BOSSINESS
HUMOR	DISSIPATION

"I overcome"

Negative Metal, Yang

Great wisdom and authority characterize the Taurean born in Rooster years. This person will he self-possessed in the extreme. Taurus endows him with unshakable determination. Rooster lends enthusiasm and blind faith. From an early age, the Taurus/Rooster exhibits a tendency to dominate. Taurus/Roosters are, however, not usually political leaders. These folks do not ever try to get elected to office by popular vote, cheered at the football game for their team spirit or even hailed as the "best mom or dad in the world" by their kids. Taurus/Rooster is quite simply, fearlessly and naturally prominent.

Preeminence does not have to mean tyranny. Taurus/Rooster is not interested in running the lives or careers or the spiritual lives of others for the sake of wielding power. Yet, because of their exceptional mettle, Taurean Roosters are often found in high places. Water seeks its own level. Even if one wanted to, it would be impossible to relegate this feisty person to an inferior rank. Subordination does not just make Taurus/Roosters crazy and neurotic and angry the way it might a Taurus/Ox. Submission just doesn't fit Taurus/Roosters. Subjugation and Taurus/Rooster form an impossible juxtaposition that simply cannot exist.

Because Taurus/Roosters possess natural (not artificial, remember) power, they come by compassion easily. You will note among the Taurean Roosters of your acquaintance that in dicey situations they invariably take the side of the underdog against unfair authoritarian practices. Taurus/Rooster wants to help out people he feels are less suited for dealing with this complex life. A Taurus/Rooster can always be counted on to stick up for the little guy, back the downtrodden and tout the advantages of hiring the handicapped.

Now, due to this penchant for favoring the ill-used and rising up against the bullies of the world, Taurean/Roosters sometimes lose themselves in personal causes or vendettas in the name of another, less fortunate soul. What starts out as pity or charity can wax into passion. If he doesn't watch out, before he knows it, the Taurus/Rooster is locked into a very unhealthy love relationship. Underdogs have a funny way of secretly wishing to be masters. Within the confines of a love affair or even a friendship, secrets will out. I have known some Taurus/Roosters, basically outwardly dominant people, whose wills have been broken by an underdog/bully. The strong are perhaps ineffably attracted to the weak. Sympathy is a lovely sentiment. But beware, Taurus/Rooster, don't let yourself be buffaloed by simpering ne'er-do-wells. Of course you should help people in need. But try not to let them slip between your sheets.

In personal style, Taurus/Roosters typify what I like best about the countryside. Earthiness, solidity, purity, sensuality and generosity. Taurus/Rooster is gifted for maintaining order in nature's chaos. And this person's character provides just the proper amount of steely agility to carry his coherent projects into effect.

Taurus/Roosters may have an eating problem. I've never known a skinny one. The Taurean tinge of gluttony combined with Rooster's enthusiastic adventurousness naturally makes for a certain Epicureanism. Taurus/Roosters are conscientious people, so they know how to diet and discipline themselves. But the leaning is toward the good—maybe just a smidgen too good—life.

Taurean/Roosters are substantial people. Despite all appearances (a certain cockiness and garish dress habits), these people are deeply, densely, irremediably conservative. And they are often very, very bright. For a Taurus/Rooster to skip the first four grades nr primary school and enter Harvard at age twelve is practically status quo. And it isn't just their intelligence that pushes them either. Taurus/Roosters don't particularly need social chitchat and are not upset if they don't fit in with groups. As they are intrinsically head and shoulders above others, their precocious successes, gained in a thoroughly independent fashion, are many.

Rooster's resilience is compromised in Taureans born under its influence. The Taurus is an emotional reservoir. Feelings embed themselves so profoundly under their sensitive skins that even being born a bouncy Rooster can't save them from occasional periods of frightening gloom. Loss, separation, partings and even just change really jar Taurus/Roosters. They ruminate and scratch about in the dirt and sulk and weep and brood. Only time heals the wounds Taurus/Rooster feels so achingly. Time and affection—and plenty of serious hard work.

Love

Although Taurus/Roosters are serious as a rule and not attracted to frivolity, their choice of love partners often hints at the contrary. Roosters born Taurus like to be amused. Their lives are serious enough as it is. They feel they want some levity in a partner. You will often see a strong Taurus/ Rooster whose companion is a limp-wristed wisp of a thing who doesn't stop blabbing and smiles a lot. "What does she see in that boob?" you may wonder. Fun. Hilarity. Enjoyment. Pleasure, Silliness. Lightheartedness. Joy. All the elements which are missing from the Taurus/Rooster's solemn nature.

Taurus/Roosters are faithful, to a point. They are not the syrupy falling about, I-can't-live-without-you types who promise undying physical exclusivity. No. The Taurus/Rooster is above that. But involvements and emotional attachments do grab the Taurus/Rooster's heartstrings and are not readily dislodged. His passions run deep. Should a Taurus/Rooster err a bit while away on a business trip, you can be sure that she'll come home just as in love with her lifetime partner as when she got on the airplane last Tuesday. These people are not given to abandonment of true affection.

Should you love a Taurus/Rooster, you must be careful not to weigh too heavily on their seemingly unflinching souls. These people appear more emotionally tough than they really are. If you see a black cloud float in and hover over your Taurus/Roosters head, engendering a week-long silent sulk, you must be brave. Get the best food and drink around. Have a candlelight dinner ready when Taurus/Rooster arrives and wait till he's just a wee bit tipsy. Then talk. And talk fast. Ask what's wrong. Insist. Show your compassion. Be amusing. Wear your heart on your sleeve. Taurus/Roosters need to cry too. But they don't like to admit it. It's up to you to bring out their emotions – and the Kleenex box.

Compatibilities

Your greatest affinities are with Cancer, Virgo and Capricorn people born in Ox, Dragon or Snake years. You'll also find Pisces alluring in their Ox or Snake form. Don't dally with Leo/Cats or Leo/Roosters. Their vanities clash with your own. Aquarius and Scorpio/Dogs and Cats are not your favorite house pets either. Too much competition for authority.

Home and Family

In all matters pertaining to what is serious and profound, the Taurean Rooster is a champ. Family life, with all of its intricately braided emotional patterns and tics, pleases old Taurus/Rooster right down to the ground. The more kids the merrier. The more parties and birthdays and bar mitzvahs and weddings they can throw, the happier they'll be. Taurus/Roosters like to be entertained, cajoled, brought along to enjoying themselves. They make a perfect audience for all manner of family skits and shenanigans.

As a sibling, cousin, aunt or uncle, Taurus/Rooster is also right up there with the best. As Taurus/Roosters take duty seriously. they never forget to phone an aging relative or remember to celebrate Mother's Day for their maiden aunt's sake. They are likewise disappointed in family members who don't accept their offerings of affection and aid. Taurus/Roosters are bossy people. I wouldn't want to have a Taurus/Rooster mother-in-law.

Taurus/Rooster children are strong-minded. Tough but adorable. Resilient but sentimental. To do right by one of these very special kids, the parent should try to provide an atmosphere of learning, growing, building and knowing. The Taurus/Rooster child's seemingly independent spirit requires far more cuddling and nurturing than he or she lets on. Always tuck them in at bedtime, read them stories, nuzzle their necks and remind them how much they are loved.

Profession

There is nothing a Taurus/Rooster cannot do—except be relegated to subordinate positions. All jobs where authority is needed will suit this character's needs. The Taurus/Rooster can also run his or her own business without any trouble whatsoever. Law, medicine, scholarly pursuits—all of these will work. The Taurus/Rooster is a capable sort.

And not only is this character able, he is gifted for earning a living. I don't think he is the type to end up rich. Taurus/Roosters don't much care about wealth. They like to be comfortable. But they're not interested in money for its own sake. But work is the Taurus/Rooster's friend. He loves to perform well in whatever he does. As failure cannot be taken lightly by such a Spartan soul as Taurus/Rooster, he usually doesn't allow himself to go under. Circumstances can, however, get beyond his control. And when they do, Taurus/Rooster tries desperately to re-create order to stem the tide of inevitability. His efforts are valiant.

You can trust the failed Taurus/Rooster to struggle back up the ladder to find a new, way to get ahead and satisfy his need for prowess. Nothing really daunts this person forever. But the uphill trudge will be both long and hard. We are not exactly dealing with a butterfly.

Suitable careers for Taurean born Roosters are: Writer, leader, musician, actor, journalist, real estate magnate.

Famous Taurus Roosters: Rod McKuen, Peter Townshend, Annie Dillard, Andrei Sakharov, Catherine of Russia, Craig David, Daniel Gélin, Danielle Fishel, Jessica Alba, Otto Klemperer, Renee Zellweger.

	TAURUS		DOG

ARDOR	LANGUOR	CONSTANCY	UNEASINESS
DETERMINATION	PREJUDICE	UNSOCIABILITY	CRITICISM
INDUSTRY	INTRACTABILITY	RESPECTABILITY	DUTY
PATIENCE	GLUTTONY	SELF-RIGHTEOUSNESS	CYNICISM
LOGIC	COMPLACENCY	INTELLIGENCE	HEROISM
SENSUALITY	JEALOUSY	TACTLESSNESS	MORALITY

"I have"

Earth, Venus, Fixed

"I worry"

Positive Metal, Yang

Here is a dutiful combination gifted for performances of all kinds and cursed by a surfeit of uneasiness, which easily translates into dissatisfaction. Let me explain. Tanreans born in Dog years tend to complain a lot. They find fault with much of what life offers, As for what life doesn't offer—they feel it should. Taurus/Dogs have an overdeveloped sense of injustice. They cannot understand why it seems as if the cards are always stacked against them. Why are others so lucky? Why do things seem to just fall into their laps? Why don't wonderful lucky things happen to me? grumbles the dissatisfied Taurus/Dog.

Childlike appeal and apparent innocence of all that is tawdry and crooked make the Taurean Dog a lovable and dear companion. He's interested in and capable of many different pursuits. He usually has a talent for amusing crowds and is willing and able to take on great responsibilities. Despite his inborn talent for determination and respectability, for industry and even heroism, the Taurus/Dog suffers from a painful lack of self-confidence. He is never, from childhood forward, quite sure of himself. Often, because of this insecurity, the Taurus/Dog settles for remaining in the wings of life for the whole or his childhood and adolescence. Then, by the time he is old enough to answer his cue and leap onto center stage, Taurus/Dog may not feel quite ready yet. He'll hang back, find excuses for delaying his one-man show and, if he not careful to find the right partner who pushes and prods and loves and cares enough to shove the Taurus/Dog out there, the Taurus/Dog may find himself at retirement age standing hangdog in the same wings of life wondering whatever happened to his cue.

This person is a natural-born worry wart He's also extremely perfection conscious and wants things to be done right and go well and come out flawless. If they don't, he will be the first to blame not only himself but also to scold those who surround him. "Why don't you take things more seriously?" wonders Taurus/Dog to his lighthearted friend or mate or child. "Why can't you see how important this is?" he may chide.

When the Taurus/Dog does succeed in a big way, he may tend toward smugness. He feels he has worked harder than others to get where he is. He knows that some people might have cheated or tricked to get places in life. But not the Taurean Dog. Never! Taurean Dogs are the first to consider themselves "good" people who always do things "right." Struggle and huff and puff and bark and growl and sweat. Then, when they do win fame or fortune or the approval of their entourage, Taurus/Dogs are capable of opining, "I deserve this. I work harder than anybody else. It's about time somebody recognized my enormous talent."

You see, life really is not easy for Taurus/Dogs. Because of their own reticent attitude, they often are left out, overworked, and misunderstood.

They are more conscientious than lots of other folks. And they are sensitive in the extreme. Couple this sensitivity with a native tendency to jealousy and possessiveness and you come up with a mighty testy character. You may see the Taurean Dog as inexcusably self-involved. But don't think for one minute that lie perceives himself as anything less than Albert Schweitzer—caring, loving, giving, warmhearted, kind, indulgent.

Taurus/Dogs do take up causes and care a lot about the little guy. They are liberal-hearted and willing to go far to help out the less fortunate. This person can persevere in what seems to be hopeless situations. His loving and caring capacity is very, very strong.

Usually, these people are generous and willing literally to give you the shirt off their backs. They are sweet-natured underneath all that ill-tempered blather and dither. Taurus/Dogs are the kinds of dogs who growl a lot when they first meet you and who, before you know it, have jumped into your lap and are licking your face all over. They need encouragement and plenty of applause.

Love

The doubting Dog nature coupled with the plodding and stubborn yet possessively ardent Taurus personality provides us with a constant, faithful and sincerely devoted lover. No mountain is too high to climb, no river too wide to wade across for the sake of this person's love object. In relationships, the Taurus/Dog always feels that he is the one who gives the most. And he likes it that way.

What Taurean Dog people sometimes fail to take into consideration is that in order to be able to love them back with the identical fervor they throw into each affair, their partner must be possessed of abnormally superior powers of tickle. To be the full-time lover of a snappy and grave Taurus/Dog, you have to be a stand-up comic, a Saint-Bernard and a clown. The successful mate for Taurus/Dogs is able to find humor in all aspects of things. Otherwise, what with the natural Taurean Dog pessimism turned up full volume for life, the household ambience may amount to something akin to a cemetery's. Bottom line: if you love a Taurus/Dog, always keep 'em laughing.

Compatibilities

Love will blossom between you and Cancer, Virgo, Capricorn and Pisces/ Cats, Horses and Tigers. Blends like the above suit your testy and essentially pessimistic nature. You need to be buoyed, optimized and occasionally booted in the rear end, too. But not by Leo, Scorpio or Aquarius/Tigers, Dragons or Goats. Their motives may not be wholly altruistic. Yours usually are.

Home and Family

The Taurus/Dog will not make a great fuss about his surroundings. He usually likes things efficient and warmly colored. But whether or not he has the latest in designer furnishings is of little consequence. Rather than fussing about the latest or the best in modern or antique design, the Taurus/Dog will want things personalized his way. He may move the furniture around in a hotel room or tack up magazine pictures on the walls of a rented vacation flat. He likes things to be quaint and cozy and comfortable. He eschews plastics.

The Taurus/Dog's family, even though it is often a source of immense disappointment to him from the beginning of his life, ranks high on his popularity meter. Where there is a need for devotion and duty and a call for duty and reliability, you can always count on the services of this loyal cohort. Where his children are concerned, he will be both careful and serious. He may be a tiny bit strict with kids, but it's only because he wants them to be happier than he ever was and the Taurus/Dog firmly believes that self-restraint is one of the secrets of happiness. You watch. If a Taurus/Dog ever dares to indulge himself in any debauchery at all, the guilt and self-recrimination are shattering to witness. He wants to be thought of as above reproach.

The Taurus/Dog child will strike you as rather solemn at first. He is not easy to know and requires lots of cheering up and jollying along. This child can be counted on to obey and to try to do things the way parents wish. If you have such a kid, look for his own personal passion very early on and force him to overcome shyness and trepidation, so that later on he will have fewer chances to moan about what he missed. Get him out of the shadows at a young age.

Profession

There is little the Taurus/Dog cannot accomplish, He is usually both talented and willing to work. He may prove slower to achieve than others, but the fine results will always be worth the extra time he spends. Dogs born in Taurus will be both reliable and concerned about the impression made on colleagues and clients. As he may be a touch awkward socially, the Taurean Dog must be careful to surround himself with outgoing and gregarious colleagues. Taurus/Dogs are good at detail, and although not exactly influenceable, they are definitely open to new ideas and always ready to try out more modern methods.

As an employee, the Taurus/Dog will be loyal and forthright. From time to time he may prove a shade argumentative over niggling little points. But on the whole Taurean Dogs take care to see a job well done. As bosses, Taurus/Dogs enjoy a good reputation among their workers. The Taurean Dog, remember, is a fair person and, even if a tiny bit grouchy sometimes, is overall a kindly sort who doesn't mind sharing the less pleasant tasks with his colleagues. If cheated or tricked in business deals, the Taurus/Dog may grow bitter. He doesn't take kindly to con jobs. So, if you were thinking of trying to hoodwink a Taurus/Dog, remember that his bite is almost as harsh as his bark, I can see Taurean Dogs in all sorts of jobs. They might be physicists or city planners or own and operate a newspaper store or bookstore. Show business and politics alike present the Taurus/Dog with opportunities to use his talents well. He'll be very fulfilled as a teacher or in any rural job requiring attention to ecological concerns.

Some famous Taurus/Dogs: Lenin, Golda Meir, Shirley MacLaine, Andre Agassi, Arletty, Carl XVI (King of Sweden), Cher, Georges Moustaki, Master P. Michel Poniatowski, Scott Bairstow, Serge Reggiani, Socrates, Uma Thurman, Yannis Xenakis.

TAURUS

ARDOR	LANGUOR
DETERMINATION	PREJUDICE
INDUSTRY	INTRACTABILITY
PATIENCE	GLUTTONY
LOGIC	COMPLACENCY
SENSUALITY	JEALOUSY

"I have"

Earth, Venus, Fixed

PIG

SCRUPULOUSNESS	CREDULITY
GALLANTRY	WRATH
SINCERITY	HESITATION
VOLUPTUOUSNESS	MATERIALISM
CULTURE	GOURMANDISM
HONESTY	PIGHEADEDNESS

"I civilize"

Negative Water, Yin

You are likely to find one of these subjects among the "beautiful people." Taureans born in Pig years, albeit rather rustic in certain ways, are attracted to the upper levels of society. Material wealth will serve to embellish the opulent life of the Taurean/Pig. He enjoys both riches and position and, frankly. never accepts less than what he feels is his absolute due (lots). This person is also quite bossy. He needs to have his own way. He will cooperate. But only if he gets to be the "Mommy."

The types of activities that can be undertaken by a Taurus/Pig are myriad. No task or chore is too difficult for his brute force. No fine detailed work with needle, brush or knife defies his deftness. This is a big sign, both generous and loving in the extreme, hardworking and very down-to-earth.

The Taurean born Pig may not have a sparkling youth or a smooth, harmonious adolescence. But when he grows up, the Taurus/Pig deliberately sets out to find his lost chords, to put order and concord back into his tumultuous lire. Methodically and with great thought and care, the Taurus/Pig finds the people with whom he will share his life, takes great pains to protect and make them comfortable in luxurious surroundings, and then grippingly, fervently, solidly loves them.

Taurus/Pigs are very often handsome people whose grace, despite the avoirdupois that both Bull and Porky summon in the mind's eye, is lovely to watch. They are tough and dense people. But Taurus/Pigs are rarely severe or unkind, cruel or unfair to others. They truly like their fellow man and are seldom, if ever, thoroughly disgruntled.

Combine the logic and patience of the Taurus with the scrupulous sincerity of the Pig and you have a limpid, sterling character. This person will readily share his material wealth, and draw up and carry out huge serious projects. And his word is as good as law—better. He honors his contracts and is fraught with terrible self-doubt and worry if for some reason he cannot.

Because the Taurus/Pig is essentially such a pure soul, always willing to give ears and tail to cooperate with others, it follows that sometimes he is also extremely influenceable. I mean, if a Taurus/Pig believes in somebody, buys someone's act all the way, then his faith and loyalty to that person will be unshakable. If, unfortunately, the "someone" in question is a rotten egg and drags the poor good-hearted Taurus/Pig into treachery and crime, it will be the moral and emotional undoing of our hero.

Taurean Pigs don't like to be rude to others. But if they are pushed too far, they will read their tormentor the riot act in no uncertain terms. Like all Pigs, this one puts up with a lot. But when they are pushed to the limit and have been taken advantage of one time too many, Taurus/Pigs charge full steam ahead into the fray, vituperating like wet hens. Trust me, nobody wants to be told off by an enraged Taurean born in a Pig year.

Powerful these people are. And impenetrable as well. They love company and are always the ones who shop and cook and make lovely dinners where people remember having such a roaring good time. But when they are working or just thinking, you need a power-driven crowbar to enter their concentration aura. This ability to persevere alone, nibbling slowly every day at a huge amount of work, is what gives the Taurus/Pig his ticket to success. Everything this person does is tinged with victory.

Love

When it comes to knowing how to love, romance, tenderness, loyalty and depth of feeling are true qualities. Taurus/Pigs have them all. They are really all-or-nothing love bugs with a unique taste for the finest that sensuality has to offer. These types adore food and don't even mind tippling a bit. Their homes are invariably comfortable and richly appointed. The entire ambience speaks of occasions for amorous activity. Large bedrooms, draped in velvets, and tinted lampshades entice the loved one into a nest whence he or she is not likely to exit intact.

Taurean Pigs crave beauty and comfort. They require a lot of chatting and foreplay, appreciate lavish gifts and elegant parties. Don't invite a Taurus/Pig to come and stay with you in a hut or a tent. These subjects really hate to rough it. Give a Taurus/Pig a luxurious villa on the French Riviera or a sprawling palazzo in Tuscany. Invite him to stay on a huge ranch in Texas. But don't ask a Taurus/Pig to love you unless you're willing and able to help provide at least one of the above.

You will need to arm yourself with patience, too. Taurus/Pigs get things done but they love to take their time. If they are busy playing a piano sonata when they're supposed to be at an appointment, Taurus/Pigs will finish the music first. Taurus/Pigs are also mild people. They don't go for exaggerated, mawkish knight-in shining-armor behavior. Never serenade a Taurus/Pig under his window or swashbuckle around him.

He'll only laugh and you may never get to see that cozy nest I was talking about earlier. Be cool. And intelligent. And funny.

Compatibilities

Pursue a Capricorn or Cancer/Cat, Dragon or Goat for the purposes of happiness ever after. For some hanky-panky you might be amused by a bout with a sexy Virgo or Pisces/Goat character. Your sensitivities match up perfectly. But if you want some future with your sensuality, stick with Cats and Dragons of the Cancer, Virgo, Capricorn or Pisces persuasion. Both Chinese signs are capable of true complicity with you. Don't waste any time on Leo/Snakes or Monkeys. Steer around Scorpio/Tigers, Roosters and Dogs. Whatever yon do, don't go getting involved with Aquarius/Snakes, Roosters or Monkeys.

Home and Family

The call of duty is music to the ears of Taureans born Pig, Relatives are always welcome at their homes, family reunions are often held in their backyards, and when cousin Sara gets married it's usually good old Taurus/Pig who throws the reception at his place. Taurus/Pigs faithfully phone their aging parents and listen to hours of woeful tales with an indulgent smile on their lips.

As parents themselves, Taurus/Pigs may be incidentally bossy, but they are not very authoritarian. They like to think they are giving leeway to their kids, room to grow and imagine and learn about art and culture. Taurus/Pigs are themselves very artistic people. The thought that their child might feel constrained or restricted by stodgy teachers or dumb rules irks the Taurus/Pig. He'll be the first parent to summarily remove his kid from any stuffy environment where the child is unhappy.

Taurus/Pig children are rich in spirit. They don't mind sharing their games or letting other kids borrow their bikes. But little Taureans born in Pig years often insist on having their own way. Their angers are few but when they arise they amount to real bite-the-rug tantrums. This child needs a comfortable and secure environment in which to develop his artistic side. Take him to museums and the ballet, shower him with affection and don't be shy of encouraging self-discipline. He will respect rigor as long as it is combined with true caring.

Profession

This person will be talented for professions requiring diligence, strength, artistic appreciation and a sense of team spirit. Taurus/Pigs are not loners. They crave company and like to feel as though they "belong" where they work.

As a coworker, the Taurus/Pig will probably strike others as slightly on the demanding side. He is stubborn and when an idea sticks in his brain, he doesn't let go of it easily. I feel sorry for anyone who tries to take his position away or one-up the Taurus/Pig in a chain of command. This person has a natural penchant for surpassing others.

Appropriate jobs for the Taurus/Pig are: executive, museum curator, artist, university administrator or professor, art dealer, antiques expert, giant of industry or even politician.

Successful Taurean Pigs: Fred Astaire, Vladimir Nabokov, Oliver Cromwell, David Boreanaz, Guy de Cars, James Buchanan, Laurent Cabrol, Luciano Benneton, Maureen O'Sullivan, Patrick Bruel, and the empire-builder William Randolph Hearst.

Other books by Suzanne White

CHINESE ASTROLOGY PLAIN AND SIMPLE

THE NEW ASTROLOGY

LA DOUBLE ASTROLOGIE

LA DOBLE ASTROLOGIA

THE NEW CHINESE ASTROLOGY

LA NEUVA ASTROLOGIA CHINA

THE ASTROLOGY OF LOVE

LADYFINGERS (A NOVEL)

BALD IN THE MERDE (A NOVELETTE)

Available in all formats (ebook and paper) from all Booksellers

Personal Telephone Readings, Books, Chapters, Horoscopes and Lifestyle
Advice at http://www.suzannewhite.com

Made in the USA
Las Vegas, NV
16 April 2023

70680356R00039